The
Bold Adventure

Ian Nimmo

125 years of Teesside and the Evening Gazette

Pacesetter . . . 125 years after the launch of the Evening Gazette the newspaper remains a winner. Editor Ranald Allan accepts a plaque from Michael Brown, president of the Thomson Corporation, to mark winning the Thomson Regional Newspapers Campaigning Paper of the Year award in 1994.

First published in Great Britain by

The Breedon Books Publishing Company Limited
44 Friar Gate, Derby, DE1 1DA.
1994.

Copyright Evening Gazette, Middlesbrough, 1994.

ISBN 1 873626 88 6

Printed and bound by Hillman Printers, Frome, Somerset.
Cover printed by BDC Printing Services Limited of Derby

Evening Gazette

CONTENTS

This small stained glass window is one of the few relics from the Gazette's days in Zetland Road. It was used as an ornament set in the the door of the manager's office and depicts an old-time printing method long before the Gazette was born.

Acknowledgements

The co-operation and help of a great many people made this book possible. It is written to mark the *Evening Gazette's* 125th anniversary. I was privileged to be the assistant editor — and later editor — of the paper when it celebrated its centenary in 1969. It has therefore been most rewarding to meet and work again with some old colleagues during my research.

In particular, I would like to thank: present editor, Mr Ranald Allan, for all his help and kindness, along with his resourceful personal assistant, Kath Taylor; hard working-librarian Barbara Thompson; David Whinyates, David Lorimer and Dave Jamieson, *Gazette* editorial professionals from my past; Gordon Fairbairn and Eric Paylor of the sports desk; Mike Morrissey and old friend and former editor Bill Sinclair for checking some of the manuscript; my wife Grace for her hawkeye with proof reading and son Struan, who was born in Middlesbrough General Hospital, for his ready assistance; my gratitude to Teesside writers, journalists and photographers, past and present, who have touched on the story of the *Gazette* and the area in books and articles and to those many people who have provided information, advice and encouragement. Thank you all.

Ian Nimmo
July, 1994.

A Remarkable Man

IN 1869, when the *Evening Gazette* was born, Queen Victoria reigned. William Gladstone was Prime Minister, Canada had just become a Dominion and the Suez Canal was opened with a flourish. A rumour whispered around Europe that the Franco-Prussian War was brewing, in South Africa the Zulus were taking up their assegais again; and at the other side of the world the West was still being won from the Red Indians. Dodge City had still not even heard of Wyatt Earp, and the American Civil War had been over for only four years.

On Teesside the iron rush was at full sweat, the roaring furnaces usurping the power from the late great king coal, gouging a surge of industrial life from the Clevelands that eventually led to unprecedented development, sending the population soaring and the name of Middlesbrough ringing throughout the country. Sadly, attendant on the new-found wealth of this "infant Hercules", as Gladstone called the burgeoning Middlesbrough, was the aching poverty and misery that so often is prosperity's grim companion on the first and second stages of boom expansion.

Beggars whined in the streets and in Stockton they were menacing. Battles and brawls with the police were commonplace. Gambling was at feverpoint and two 14-

Hugh Gilzean Reid . . . from Scotland to success

year-olds caught playing pitch-and-toss in Dacre Street were given a deterrent six lashes each. Shops were selling whisky at 16s a gallon, gin at 12s, a fine pair of shoes for under two shillings, blouses for 8 1/2d, ladies' merino combinations for a shilling, as well as those universal salves for all ills "fine healthy pond leeches, constantly fresh".

The Zetland Hotel in Saltburn boasted

outstanding views of the German Ocean, and it cost 7s 6d to hazard your life on it by sailing to London every Wednesday.

It was into this setting that Hugh Gilzean Reid, the son of a penurious Scottish crofter arrived in search of fortune, fame if chance took it his way, and adventure.

Gilzean Reid was the founder of the *Evening Gazette* and a remarkable man. In fact, such were his achievements on so wide a platform that it is fair to say he has been undervalued by historians. Of medium height, slim, wiry, with a shock of black hair in his youth and a heavy moustache, he had a surfeit of restless and tenacious energy that would have him pacing the floor at company meetings with the long stride of the farmer, ideas and future plans bursting from him. But it was his vision and ideals combined with a certain Scottish obstinacy

that refused to be shifted from his principles, or a course once set, plus a quite exceptional humanity and understanding of his fellow men, that caught the attention when he first arrived in Teesside.

They were the qualities that took him to a knighthood for his services to journalism and journalists, to Westminster as the honourable Independent Democrat member for Aston Moor, brought him the deputy Lieutenancy of the North Riding of Yorkshire, honorary LLDs from Aberdeen and the State University of Columbia, made him first President and Fellow of the Institute of Journalists, first President of the World's Press Parliament, as well as many other glittering accolades picked up on the wayside of his astonishing career. Because he was a man who had come up the hard way, each honour conferred had particular

South Street, Middlesbrough around 1850

meaning and pleasure, for Sir Hugh also knew what it was to be a nobody and in his childhood he had been familiar with the exigencies of a half-ration diet, oatmeal and salt herring, when the purse ran dry.

The humble beginning was a thatched croft in Cruden, Aberdeenshire, where he was born in 1837. He was reared under the aegis of the celebrated Scottish tradition of hard work, a sound education and a healthy fear of God.

Times were hard. When he was only eight years old, the tiny Hughie Reid was forced to help out the family income by taking a job on a neighbouring farm, turning the handle of a hand-threshing machine for three halfpence a day, dutifully given to his mother every Saturday afternoon. She was a dedicated churchwoman, a great campaigner on behalf of the United Free Church of Scotland and no doubt her religious zeal helped to give him a serious turn of mind. But his thirst for knowledge and depth of thought even in that small community dedicated to God and learning, caused astonishment. "We were taught reading and writing", said Sir Hugh, "with glimpses of Latin and English composition; and the hard times, it may be, fitted one for the harder."

His first connection with newspapers was as a messenger boy trudging miles across the fields and moorlands to bring back the single copy of the Aberdeen *Journal* for the district. Often, to speed it on its rounds, he would read the main news to groups of eager listeners.

As the years passed, parting time drew closer, something the close-knit penurious families of Scotland knew so well and dreaded. After a marathon hike through one of the worst Highland blizzards for years, he arrived in the silver city of Aberdeen.

Although his first job was in an art printing and publishing establishment which kindled a life-long interest in art, he also managed to attend university lectures in Aberdeen and Edinburgh, and even entered theological college to train for the ministry. But at 18 the urge to write and communicate took him into journalism. It was his destiny. The *Journal* gave him a post in their Banff office and he learned fast. Indeed, his journalistic skills progressed so quickly that after working on several other Scottish newspapers, he became editor of the Edinburgh *News* in 1861 when he was still only 23. Clearly his natural skills and drive had equipped him for running his own newspaper and he returned north to establish his first title, the *Observer* in his native Buchan. But it was not long before he was taking the road that thousands of Scots had marched before and more since — the highway south to a "wider sphere of usefulness and a bigger salary".

The old Town Hall, Middlesbrough

From the *Gazette* of 1889

CONVICTIONS OF KERNOGHAN

Appeal to Quarter Sessions

The case of James Kernoghan, of Middlesbrough, which has exacted such great interest throughout the district, and in many other parts of the North of England, came before the North Riding Quarter Sessions at Northallerton today on appeal.

It will be remembered that the defendant was a foreman riveter at the shipbuilding yard of Messrs Raylton Dixon & Co., was convicted of stealing 7s 6d belonging to his employers and sentenced to three months imprisonment with hard labour.

The alleged theft was committed in connection with a system of extra payments to the shipbuilding riveters, and as the conviction touched a custom by which a large number of men here and elsewhere profited, it aroused an intense feling of excitement among the latter.

MR GLADSTONE'S VISIT

Mr Gladstone's reception in Florence has been magnified. The Florentines have vied with one another to do him honour, and all Italy has seemed anxious to commemorate the great deeds done years ago by the statesman who stood almost alone as the friend of Italy...but the average English Tory can see no good in Mr Gladstone, and can wish him nothing but harm, and the proceedings in Florence have thus in many quarters been most malignantly and ignobly assailed.

Paper Lances

THE Middlesbrough newspaper scene in those early days was a deadly jousting ground, where too many competitors snarled, snapped and tilted at each other, fighting for survival against a background of poverty and illiteracy — and increasing political awareness and loyalties. During the week these little paper knights would gather their strength and hone their newsprint lances for publication day. They were flaunting, challenging battlecries in ink, political editorial pennants streaming for all to acknowledge. Fatalities were many, but there was always another young hopeful ready to join the fray. The whole industry was in parlous state and it was not unusual for fly-by-night managements to flee their debt-ridden premises, leaving bewildered staffs whistling for their money.

Gilzean Reid, aged 28 years, looked at this scene long and objectively. Against the backdrop of the thrusting Teesside, he came to the conclusion that he liked what he saw, the thriving industry, the increasing importance of Tees as a port, the rising population, the buoyant growth wherever he cast his eye.

Most of all, with the knowledge that he could produce a better newspaper than any that existed in the area at the time, he liked his carefully-calculated vision for the future — the rich commercial potential and the role that he himself could play with his own particular talents in the making of Teesside. For him, with a background of Highland crofts and girning poverty, it was an exciting, adventurous, personal challenge.

This is where a man can make something of his life, he said, and at the same time,

with hard work and the guidance of God, help in some way to improve the conditions and education of his fellow men.

He wasted no time. In 1865 he negotiated for and bought the struggling *Weekly Gazette and Times*, with a sagging circulation of 700 copies a week — and he set to with a will to make it the best newspaper in the country, published from his office at 104 High Street, Stockton, and with the help of four men and two boys, printed at the *Gazette* office, Railway Crossing, Middlesbrough.

It was an inauspicious start, but this was the forefather of today's modern *Evening Gazette* with its army of daily readers.

Regrettably, much of the information of those early times has been lost for ever, for all the *Gazette* files before 1866 were destroyed in an office fire, along with the first five issues of *The Daily Gazette*, when it was launched in 1869. The earliest record of the newspaper's birth is described by Charles Postgate in his "History of Middlesbrough", although even he is vague.

This is what he had to say: "Sometime after the *Middlesbrough News* started (in 1855), a new weekly Liberal paper called the *Weekly Gazette* came into existence, followed by a daily of the same name. A Conservative journal, the *Weekly Exchange,* followed, the proprietors also publishing a daily issue. Both the latter, however, succumbed to adverse fate, and left the *Gazette* in undisputed possession of the field."

Then William Lillie, former Borough Librarian and local historian, reports in his

Middlesbrough history: "At Stockton on 30th December 1859 there was issued the *Stockton Gazette and Teesside Advertiser,* and at Middlesbrough Jordison's *Middlesbrough Times*. It has been stated that H. G. Reid purchased the paper in 1865, which is probably true as he went to Stockton on newspaper business. It is certain that by 9th January, 1867, he was in possession of both papers, for on that date he published a paper called *The Middlesbrough and Stockton Gazette and General Advertiser for the North of England.*"

Although Gilzean Reid was determined to make a commercial success of his launch into daily publication, his editorial objectives were commendably clear. Beyond all other considerations he would make his *Daily Gazette* serve the community —and he dedicated himself and his paper to that aim.

He would reflect, he stated, the people of Teesside, their lives, interests, fears, problems, opinions and aspirations. And because Gilzean Reid was a man of unusual sensitivity and humanity, as well as being a talented journalist, he resolved to use his paper as a vehicle of campaign against the over-burdening pressures on the lot of the working class in this new industrial El Dorado, as well as against many of the social evils of the day that had gathered in force and kept pace with the fast-growing township.

With a pronouncement of intent that was also a challenge to his rivals, Gilzean Reid declared that he would serve his readers loyally, speak out for their rights and defend them when necessary and show courage and honesty and firmness of purpose as he reported factually and dependably. This was the code of a man of the highest ideals and principles. He set it out as a guide to the operation of the paper in 1869. It has remained the code of the *Evening Gazette* ever since along with its campaigning style on behalf of its readers.

When the time came to launch his *Daily Gazette*, it became clear Gilzean Reid had

THE forged letters which so nearly set Russia and Germany at war have now been published, and they certainly seem to have been clumsily executed, though cleverly conceived. They made our Prince Bismarck to have been a very indifferent sort of diplomatic liar. The deception at which they hinted, was of a very mean and unworthy kind.

—North Eastern Weekly Gazette, January 7, 1888

chosen his moment well. The advertisement and stamp taxes had finally been discarded, and although the population of Middlesbrough was then only 30,000 it was visibly increasing every year. The build-up of pressure to force better and fuller education was beginning to mount, further progressing the potential readership, for at that time as many as 12 per cent of adults could not read at all, and many more were considerably limited.

Even by modern standards it was a magnificent marketing operation, but Gilzean Reid had still a trump card to play. The price. He believed if he could make his new *Gazette* the best paper — as well as the cheapest — it must surely succeed.

He took courage by the ears and with a deep breath and a prayer he bravely pioneered the first halfpenny evening newspaper in Britain — "all the local and latest telegraphic news" tightly packed into four well-advertised pages. He was still only 31 years of age.

The first issue of the new *Daily Gazette* appeared on Middlesbrough streets on the afternoon of November 8, 1869.

This is what it said of itself after only 14 days publication:

"We are not surprised that some of our weekly contemporaries should endeavour to produce the impression that *The Daily Gazette* was only commenced for a temporary purpose and having, as they allege, served that purpose, it must cease to exist. Even the uninitiated can understand that playing at daily papers would be a rather serious matter, and those who know what they are doing are not likely to enter upon such costly experiments.

"*The Daily Gazette* was commenced earlier than we intended with the conviction that it was needed, and our expectations, both in respect of circulation and advertising, have been more than realised. To advertisers for the week we will be able to guarantee a circulation of nearly 15,000, and when our arrangements for delivery and distribution are completed, we have every reason to expect a steady and reliable expansion.

"Our telegraphic intelligence is much more perfect than that in most of our contemporaries, and we certainly deserve some credit for publishing every evening in this locality, the news of the day from all parts of the world, and thus supplying the night previous the same intelligence, to a large extent that appears in the morning papers. There is still, however, room for improvement. The shipping department, for instance, cannot, for a few days, be what is intended; but we shall do our utmost to meet, in respect to latest intelligence, local reports and other matters, the growing requirements for this great district."

In a leading article, *The Gazette* thanked the public for their generous and spontaneous reception of the first efforts.

"As it is impossible for us to acknowledge otherwise the numerous letters of congratulations we have received from all parts of the district and from many distant parts of the country, we would here express our thanks for the kind words of encouragement and expressions of approval that have reached us during the last few days. It is needless to say that commencing a daily newspaper is a very arduous and responsible undertaking, and perfection is not to be looked for at once.

"Still, we feel — and are grateful that others whose opinions we value, and whose support we look for are ready to testify — that we have produced a daily paper not unworthy of this great district. To those contemporaries in the North and across the Border, who have spoken well of our new enterprise, we would thus publicly make our acknowledgements."

Breaky-Neck Yard, Stockton, which led between the High Street and the river . . . around 1900.

Voice of the People

SO THE "bold adventure", as Gilzean Reid put it, was launched, and by the end of November, *The Daily Gazette* had made such healthy strides that it looked the fittest paper in the area, and the readers began to flock to it. Quickly it built up a reputation for being a fearless and independent exponent of democratic principle that reached far outside its North-east environs and it was soon recognised as one of the highest forms of provincial journalism in the country. With the help of pungent editorials *The Daily Gazette* rapidly became the kind of newspaper Gilzean Reid had dreamed about, an inspiration and leader in the community in all forms of social, political and commercial life.

The *Gazette* in those early days had certainly no inhibitions about speaking its mind, although the laws of libel were hardly so stringent then. Because rivalry and competition were so fierce that the merest sign of weakness could be misconstrued as the death rattle and even precipitate an early demise, newspapers hit hard and fast and often and were all too ready to attack each other. Take for example the *Stockton Herald*, a quick-shooting weekly that blazed at everything as *The Daily Gazette* was launched. It took a potshot at the *Gazette* for "openly and avowedly advocating a bridge across the Tees". The Gazette fired back with a column-and-a-half leader which began "Every village has its buffoon, and few towns lack their eccentricity. Those people in Stockton who read that rarity in journalism called the *Herald* must have enjoyed a treat on Friday night. Our contemporary was never very wise or

worthy of much consideration, but it seems now to have fairly taken leave of its senses"

Because Gilzean Reid was always a ferocious Liberal, the *Gazette* reflected his passion. During the whole of the Victorian era it seldom missed an opportunity for reducing the Tory party to political rubble. Although Sir Hugh revelled in a good fight — "We like to meet foemen worthy of our steel" — in those early days the *Gazette* was decidedly a pacifist paper. "Is it a noble thing to mow down battalions of men by grapeshot, for one man to drive his bayonet through the heart of another. . .?" it asked of the Franco-Prussian War.

On the local front and between partisan editorials belabouring the Tories, the *Gazette* fulfilled its "determination to exercise a wholesome influence on the social life of the community, and stimulate political and industrial activity". At the height of the smallpox epidemic of 1871, when 202 citizens died, and the *Gazette* was printed on impregnated paper, it campaigned vigorously against "the glaringly defective sanitary conditions of Middlesbrough. The time has gone by for trifling with the health of the people", it pronounced censoriously.

Nor was it afraid to take the nation to task, counselling that "our military and commercial descent has been no less degrading than our political decay". Which might have been written today. "It is a symptom of a prosperous period that we should hear of so many strikes . . . the practice of arbitration has at last broken down."

Towards the end of the century, the

Middlesbrough's beginnings ... a rural scene around 1836.

Gazette developed a fiery social conscience on behalf of the working classes, pressing for "laws which defend the weak against the strong".

Radical reform was again the keynote of the editorial of June 21, 1887, Queen Victoria's Jubilee: "The monarchy must be cleansed of many of its excesses . . . the Crown must prove its value and necessity."

While jingoists could hardly wait to get to the Boer War at the turn of the century, the *Gazette* found it difficult to beat the drum. The paper was cool on hot war, except when it came to ending it: "Modern warfare is becoming increasingly recognised as an unendurable evil . . . the lovers of peace feel they have been put to shame."

The Town Council was always useful for a broadside: "The ratepayers are still responsible for a huge debt, perilously approaching £2 million — notwithstanding this debt, councillors go merrily on, adding still further to their liabilities. They pave roads with bad material, and when the ratepayers grumble they put the burden of blame on the broad shoulders of the Borough Engineer . . . the hardest day's work many government and municipal servants have to perform consists of carrying home their salary on pay day."

But, overall, town and paper had married well. The people of Teesside had their own views on matters and pressures affecting their lives and they were never dilatory in expressing them among themselves.

Now they had a voice of authority that spoke out for them when necessary and more and more began to listen with growing respect, for although there was bluntness and sometimes thunder, it was also recognised that what the *Gazette* spoke was truth and common sense and sanity. Employers, businessmen and the leaders of the district acknowledged that fact, and took heed themselves and slowly the *Daily Gazette* began to influence the thinking, then the actions and lives of the people of Teesside.

It was generally admitted that Middlesbrough was growing and shaping to the selfish demands of industry. But a town is only as big — or as little — as the people who inhabit it, and among the drudgery and filth and sweat and the aspiration it became evident that Middlesbrough had acquired a soul in the process of its growth. *The Daily Gazette* set out to nurture that soul and force space to let it grow and to expand with it. That is why the story of the *Evening Gazette* is so much the story of Middlesbrough and Teesside, for they are both inextricably linked. After all, only 16 years before the *Gazette* was launched, Middlesbrough itself was born on a little knoll beside the Tees and out of a £30,000 handshake for 500 acres of field and marshland between the selling William Chilton, of Billingham, and the prospecting Joseph Pease, industrial visionary.

Ironopolis

Bolckow and Vaughan's Ironworks, 1841

COAL, not iron, first gave Middlesbrough its life. Joseph Pease was searching for a site for a coal shipping port as an outlet for the South Durham coalfields by an extension of the Stockton-Darlington railway when he first had his vision. Few towns are built on a dream and the quiet drama of the conception is worth recording.

On August 18, 1828, Pease took a boat from the mouth of the Tees and sailed up its blue-grey waters, where the salmon were still running, and slowly moved along the unkempt banks until he came to a mound on which stood a tiny hamlet. There, after careful consideration, Pease and his five partners decided to build their new town. That night he wrote in his diary: "Imagination here had ample scope in fancying the coming day when the bare fields we were then traversing would be covered with a busy multitude and the coming and going of great ships would denote the busy seaport. Time, however must roll away many successive tides ere so important a change is effected, but what man who has considered the nature and effect of our enterprise, commerce and industry, will pretend to take his stand on this spot and point the finger of scorn at this conviction and say 'That will never be'? If such a one there be then he and I are at issue. I believe it will."

Not even Joseph Pease envisaged just how quickly those changes would take place. Ten years later Middlesbrough was a town of 5,000 inhabitants, and by 1851 it had grown to 7,631, with the hard-won accoutrements of consolidation becoming apparent: a big new dock, the dignified Church of St Hilda's, a fine town hall, and optimistic plans for the future — yet gloriously unaware of the dramatic changes ahead.

And it continued to grow, steadily in terms of the coal years, dramatically as the Cleveland iron finds hinted a new diverse prosperity, with excruciating swiftness as the sniff of quick wealth outpaced the good intentions of the planners when the great iron rush took over, casting caution to the winds, catching up the whole North-east in a fever of excitement and booming expansion.

It was unprecedented. It was extraordinary. It was impossible. But by the time the *Daily Gazette* was published, the population had leapt to 39,000 — and was rising fast.

Those quite incredible days can never be repeated. It was the partnership between the driving John Vaughan and the shrewd and moneyed William Bolckow that gave the iron rush direction, and Middlesbrough became transcended. The iron masters set the pattern. Think big, splash money, take chances, don't falter, it may lose you your shirt. The same exhilarating recklessness spirited its way to the workmen at the blast furnace and the diggings and throughout the whole industry, until the agony of overwork became almost a glorification. Toil, risk, and exhaustion; beer, food and a roof. Slave hard, play hard and tomorrow is another day.

The country had just emerged from the hungry Forties and men were ready to work for as little as 4s a day, with the blastfurnacemen on a 12-hour shift. To get a Sunday off they were required to work a 24-hour shift every alternate Sunday. But in those early times of iron fever it did not seem to matter. Sweat and drudgery had become a pride sorely earned, indolence a humiliation.

The green fields disappeared, the first of the many, gormandised by the clanging new plants, reeking monsters voraciously gobbling the rough ironstone from Grosmount, gleaned from the beaches between Saltburn and Whitby, then from that epoch-making 16-foot deep Cleveland main seam.

They set up a mighty crunching, grinding, digesting and regurgitating for a Britain suddenly gluttonous for pig iron as the industrial revolution began to flex its strength. At night the sky glowed a reflected blush red from the furnaces, and Middlesbrough mushroomed like a desert camp in an untidy, jerry-built, slummy sprawl around what for many had become the very kernel of their existence — The Works.

The Works began in a small way. Bolckow and Vaughan built their furnaces at Witton Park, but as the Cleveland deposits were tapped and the potential understood, up went three more furnaces at Eston.

> **At night the sky glowed a reflected blush red from the furnaces . . .**

The race of the iron masters was on. From Tyneside came Lowthian Bell (father of Sir Hugh Bell) and his two brothers and set up business at Port Clarence. Messrs. Gilkes, Wilson and Leatham operated from the Tees Ironworks; Messrs. Snowden and Hopkins built their Teesside blastfurnace plant; Elwon at Cleveland; Cochrane & Co at Ormesby; Sir Bernard Samuelson at South Bank. By 1855 there were 40 blast furnaces in the area, in 1861 there were 50, and by 1881 there were 156.

Although the supply at that time seemed inexhaustible, "simply a question of more shovels and more barrows", said John Vaughan, already events and discovery were overtaking the iron age so that the balance of economic advantage was tipping in favour of the conversion of raw pig iron into finished steel products, bringing its own success as the old puddling furnaces were replaced by Seimens Martin open hearth furnaces and in time led to the advent of the world-renowned Dorman Long.

Power and strength in a blast furnace

Flying Ahead

BY the time the *Daily Gazette* was first published the ironmasters not only held the whole industrial life of the area in their hands, they had also impinged into the social, political and even the scant cultural life.

Mr Bolckow was the first mayor, and became the first M.P. when the town was created a parliamentary borough in 1868. Bolckow in turn gave Albert Park to the town, a magnificent £30,000 gift. It was opened by the Duke of Connaught and the gesture brought together Bolckow and Gilzean Reid for the first time on a personal basis. It was a meeting which endured in friendship, and together, both of these remarkable men put their influence behind the striving township. Such a combination of power, industry and determination had to succeed, and it became clear that Middlesbrough, with its expanding port was well launched on the road to fame.

Behind it all was the *Gazette*, appraising, urging, pointing, encouraging, goading, roaring the direction to follow. The paper was moulding the district even as the district was moulding the paper.

Circulation was growing, revenue was rising, staff was increasing, space was cramping. The popular *Daily Gazette* had outgrown the old premises in Station Street. But there were problems. Transport was a major one. A newspaper must reach its readers with speed and with certainty — no problem today in an age of planes, trains, vans and modern technology — but horse power in those days meant exactly what it said. Horses were used to get the papers to and from the railway stations and around the

many miles of poor roads and tracks. A site near a railway was a necessity, and in 1871 the first part of the new offices went up in Zetland Road, opposite the entrance to the North Eastern Railway Station.

Still with an eye to the future, the proprietors reached for even more power to speed their printing machines, and grasped at steam, the first newspaper in the district to adopt the new system.

By 1880 a further leap in circulation created the need for even faster machines and into the new building went a Marinoni rotary press, again the first in the area, counting and clickety-clacking out 20,000 copies an hour.

The immediate problem was eased, but only temporarily. More and more readers were reaching for the *Gazette*, more and more in the outlying districts were turning to the "Voice of Middlesbrough". A second rotary was installed, then a third. The success of the *Gazette,* of course, was not automatic. Every copy had to be fought for and won against counter attack from shrewd professional competitors. Where the *Daily Gazette* had the edge was in the journalistic genius and astuteness of Sir Hugh Gilzean Reid and his choice of lieutenants.

From the beginning the paper recruited or developed men of real ability. Mr David Craig, Sir Hugh's brother-in-law from Peterhead, arrived as a lad and retired as chairman after outstanding work during the pioneering days and after the death of Sir Hugh; Mr T.P. Ritzema, whose acumen for enlightened business management was a legend, became general manager in 1875, and later manager-proprietor of the

Blackburn *Northern Daily Telegraph*, which he had helped Sir Hugh to launch; editor brothers Robert Mackie and John Mackie took over after Sir Hugh gave up the chair to concentrate on his other business interests; editor Mr A.W. Marchmont became a distinguished novelist; Manager Mr John Keeley, famed for his thrust and organising abilities, also did much public work and helped start National Savings Certificates; and, of course, there was the inimitable Mr Arthur Pickering, the anecdotic "A.P.", who joined the company in 1892 and guided the *Gazette* through plague, war, depression, expansion, strike and riot, collecting enough writs in the process, as he once said, to paper the walls of his office. In turn, he was appointed general manager, director and chairman until his retirement in 1935.

Always, of course there were problems, more and more of them, always they were solved, often ingeniously. Big news and racing results were as urgently demanded then as they are now, but in those distant days that essential modern tool of the newsroom, the telephone, was unavailable. Resourceful men on the *Gazette* were constantly on the alert for new ways and methods to speed and improve the local service to readers, and just over a century ago they came up with a winner.

It was John Keeley who first decided on recruiting a team of winged reporters — racing pigeons that could flash through the skies at speeds of more than 60 miles an hour. A pigeon cote was built in the bookbinding room and a flock of Blue

Rocks introduced and lovingly tended until they accepted their new home.

Then, like all good reporters, they set to work in their own way. In familiar *Gazette* wicker baskets off they went to West Hartlepool, Redcar, Saltburn, Stockton, Guisborough and other towns and villages. On racing days or when a news story broke, the human reporters scribbled their reports on to flimsies, fastened the paper to the pigeon's leg, then threw pigeon and news to the winds. It all proved a popular entertainment to the locals. Back at Zetland Road, Jim Clennet, bookbinder to trade, pigeon fancier at heart, kept a sharp lookout. As soon as a bird landed the flimsy was quickly detached and sped on its way to a waiting sub-editor, then on to the production chain — and there was the event recorded in the *Gazette* almost before the racegoers had left the course.

Many of the pigeons fell to sporting guns, aimed at pigeon pie especially on the hazardous West Hartlepool flight, and were sadly listed missing back at headquarters. Those little *Gazette* blue dots hurtling across Cleveland aroused great interest in the district. Middlesbrough folk were always pro-pigeon and anti-gunmen. When a blank space appeared in the Gazette where a race result should have been, readers recognised the tell-tale sign that the guns had probably been at work again, and condemned the gunmen openly.

Mr T. P. Ritzema's appointment as general manager in 1875 brought one of the keenest business minds in the country to the *Gazette* executive. Now with an eye to a future monopoly situation, he concentrated every effort into a grand slam promotion of the *Gazette* and the company's weekly papers, abandoning its printing interests to get the momentum going. Almost at once the *Gazette* took another major advance in circulation, pressing the boundaries of Teesside, more and more readers demanding the *Gazette* farther and farther from its Middlesbrough base.

Mr Ritzema was one of the first to see the significance of the trend. Backed by far-flung district editorial support, the *Daily Gazette* was seen no longer merely as the voice of Middlesbrough. Suddenly it was giving patronage to towns, villages, institutions, people and industry in an area

Lessons of the Royal Review

THE great Naval display at Spithead is said to have impressed the German emperor powerfully. The vessels of his fleet by which he was attended in British waters do not bear comparison with the powerful British ironclads. We are also assured that by so much are our ships more powerful than the Germans, by so much also our men are more dashing and skilful, and more practical. These are comfortable reflections for British readers, and especially for British taxpayers.

North Eastern Weekly Gazette, 1889

*Henry Bolckow, Ironmaster and first Mayor
of Middlesbrough*

that was increasing almost week by week, a voice of sanity and influence heard in the context of the whole of the North-east. This expanding new role was recognised on June 21, 1881, with an important announcement. "The name of this newspaper is to be changed", it said. "In future it will be called the *North-Eastern Daily Gazette* " and it was explained to readers why the step was taken.

"The gradual and permanent growth of this journal has rendered it necessary to adapt the title so as to represent the extended district over which it circulates. We have, therefore, prefixed North-Eastern as fitly expressing the area permeated by the *Gazette* and well defined by the lines of our great railway system. Not only in Middlesbrough, Stockton, the Hartlepools, Whitby, Darlington and Cleveland has the *Gazette* largely extended, but it has found its way into remote corners; and we are sparing neither effort nor expense to carry it to every available hamlet and habitation.

"With improved machinery and the best modern appliances we have been able to meet the wants of all the community, and cope successfully with formidable competition. The business and literary requirements have necessitated a direct

London agency, and we have opened a Central Office at 62 Ludgate Hill, with a manager and correspondent. Stimulated by an enlarged constituency, and liberal recognition of our efforts, we shall continue with increased vigour to promote wholesale reform, and the development and consolidation of our vast industrial interests."

What it meant was that the future of the *Gazette* was at last assured. It could look back on the struggling years with pride and the satisfaction that its aims and policies had been the right ones, enabling it to succeed and perform a service, while others had perished in the process.

Within its area the *Gazette* had become an institution. The paper had allied itself with the people in a fearless but level-headed approach that drew the praise and trust of its readers, and carried it far beyond its natural boundaries.

As for circulation, a London journal at the time set the *Gazette* sixth among the nation's provincial evening papers with 60,000 readers buying their copies every night. As for content, yet another London journal commented: " The *North-Eastern Daily Gazette* is without its peer between Manchester and Glasgow".

An old Middlesbrough fire engine

The Gazette Buildings, Zetland Road, 1871

Newspaper by Steamroller

CHEERS were added to the praise a few years later when the *Gazette* proudly boasted a new distinctive first in its field — the only newspaper in the world to be printed by steam roller.

In the early hours of November 15, 1890, an explosion in Middlesbrough gas works destroyed the gas plant, cutting off all supplies to the town, including the supply to the engines that powered the *Gazette's* printing presses. When the extent of the damage was known, members of the staff looked at each other in dismay. No power, no paper was their first thought.

But the oldest tradition in journalism is that the paper must come out. Through war, fire, flood, plague, riot — or gas explosions — the paper must be published to keep people informed. So if one source of power is turned off, a new one had to be found — and quickly!

With the merest glimmer of an outrageous idea beginning to take shape, the local authorities were contacted, with particular emphasis on roadworks, and the *Gazette's* terrible predicament explained.

Much fast talk followed, a waving of hands, eyebrows elevated, knowing winks exchanged, fingers tapping heads; much serious discussion with production managers, engineers, pick-and-shovel gangers, and at the end of it, ponderously, steadily, a giant 15-ton steam roller began to hiss and rumble its way through the streets of Middlesbrough, heading for the *Gazette* offices, a chatter of curious sightseers in procession behind it.

Up Zetland Road it clanked until at last, confronted by a thick brick wall, it could seemingly go no farther. But they were determined men on the *Gazette*, so they knocked down the wall and on the steam roller trundled into a yard owned by the Grand Hotel next door. Carefully the steamroller was manoeuvred into place against a window of the press room.

THE Maybrick case will rank with the most sensational causes celebres in the criminal annals of our land. Mrs Maybrick has been found guilty — if the verdict be a just one — and Mr Justice Stephen characterised "really horrible and dreadful a crime as ever any poor wretch who stood in the dock was accused of". The crime was that of poisoning her husband, and the obvious motive, presuming the crime to have been committed, was one of the darkest prompted by human passion that a woman, young and beautiful, well-educated, could be guilty of. The deliberate murder of the father of her three children, under such circumstances certainly casts a terrible stigma on human nature. But is her paramour not implicated in this crime?

— **1889**

Then the action really began. A long belt was passed through the window connecting the road roller with the press. Orders were shouted, men rushed, even workers erecting a new shop in Wilson Street were commandeered to help. And in due time the signal was given, the roller puffed, the wheel spun, and 64,000 copies of the *Evening Gazette* came rolling into existence. Faith had been kept with the readers, a tradition maintained.

The newspaper world cheered. Even the Americans sat up and took notice. The Detroit Free Press told its readers: "The mechanical obstacles in the way of using this unwieldy monster were great, but with the aid of a large staff of masons, fitters, joiners and trained engineering skill, together with the exercise of indomitable patience and perseverance on the part of everyone concerned, the paper was issued with the delay of only an hour. The incident caused great local excitement, but little did the readers of the paper, sitting at home, say at Berwick or Hull, perusing the full report of the gas incident, think of the engineering triumph, by which alone the publication of the paper was possible."

Said the trade journal *Iron*: "We have all heard of cracking a walnut with a steam hammer, but printing a newspaper with a road roller is a new experience."

The *Northern Daily Telegraph* commented: "The 'capturing' of the steam roller and adapting it was a marvel of newspaper genius, as the non-appearance of the *Gazette* throughout the 600 towns and villages where it circulates would have been little short of a social calamity."

The *Gazette* had made its own headlines world-wide by its ingenuity and newspapers everywhere applauded the feat.

Time for a snack at the crab and winkle stall at Stockton Market

The Exchange Inn, Middlesbrough, was the place to be seen early in the century

The country comes to town . . . Stockton Market draws the crowds in the Fifties.

Bigger and Better

THE Gazette's fame and reputation for responsible journalism was spreading fast and circulation increased with it. Once more the Gazette outgrew its premises and a new home was built adjoining the old office in Zetland Road.

On October 12, 1893, a new-look paper began to flow from its more modern headquarters, hailed as one of the finest in Britain. Once again the Gazette was looking to the future. The pages broadened, a further column was added to each. New Webb presses were introduced to produce the bigger paper, machines that not only printed 25,000 copies an hour — an incredible speed in those days — but folded them too.

To drive these monsters, two Tangye 12 horse-power gas engines were installed, housed in brick trenches set below the level of the floor to cut down risk of accident. To complete the job, a Wharfedale jobbing machine was purchased to print the news bills.

It was a newspaper fashion at the time to record the most important events of the year on coloured paper, so the *Gazette* came out on pink paper to mark the move into its splendid new home.

Unfortunately, an unforeseen snag produced a very special problem. It arrived with a roar, a rattle and a slosh. On the other side of the machine room was the Zetland Hotel, and hardly had the *Gazette's* powerful presses begun to roll as the starting lever was pulled than the vibration in the hotel cellar became so severe that the casks burst open, turning the cellar into a beery lake, barrels bobbing.

The hotel company rushed to court and obtained an injunction against the *Gazette*, effectively stopping the presses. But not for long. At all costs the paper must come out and an eight-page Hoe Press was quickly put in place, with an upper deck providing an additional four pages. The *Gazette* was back in business with hardly a stutter. Arthur Pickering introduced rubber cushioning for the embargoed machinery, and the machine room roared again, but this time with the Zetland Hotel faithful enjoying their pints in peace.

That "modern" machinery was only one of the small advance guards of a dramatic age of change that suddenly swept across the world. New thought, new inventions, new heroes, new horizons seemed to declare themselves simultaneously. It brought advances beyond the understanding of those earlier pioneers.

Electricity arrived and immediately it was clamped into harness to power industry; the telephone annihilated distance and became one of the greatest aids in the history of newspapers; and in 1899 the linotype machine revolutionised newspaper production, sweeping away much of the dreary and monotonous work of setting type and speeding the whole process of newspaper production.

Up to that time every letter, stop, space, in fact every printing symbol, had to be lifted singly from its box and set by hand, letter by letter, word by word, line by line. When printing was over, the whole process went into reverse, all the bits and pieces had to be lifted out again, washed and put back into their particular holders. The linotype ended all that. Like a giant typewriter, it clattered out the news of the day at an unprecedented rate, so that the whole setting operation and news deadlines could be rethought. The linotype machine forced a newspaper revolution of its own as the frustrating time-lag between event and publication was slashed.

At once the *Gazette* management recognised the worth of these new wonders and bought seven. They went quickly into action.

Almost daily the *Gazette* was recording history. War and rumour of war in Zululand, China, Afghanistan, Egypt, South Africa; flood, earthquake, assassination, political storm. Events that made the world gasp.

General Gordon in beleaguered Khartoum, a Bible in one hand, a sword in the other, a British force battling across the desert to save him. And, inevitably, a journalist with them. So the helios winked, the Morse tapped its message across the world, and the *Gazette's* presses thundered the disaster: "Gordon is dead, Khartoum lost".

The paper spanned the barriers of time, place and human emotion. For Teesside it was also an era of drama, irony, gloom — and boom. The iron slump of 1875, the steel bonanza of 1879. It was an age of despair and triumph, of grinding poverty, yet fortunes were lying in wait.

For a halfpenny the *Gazette* offered Teesside the complete newspaper: all the big world events, news gleaned from its own backyard and an unrivalled local commercial platform; news from the corridors of power in the places where world-shaping decisions were made —and from the Empire where the sun never set.

June 1887 saw the Jubilee of Queen Victoria, an event marked by Teessiders with their characteristic blend of fun and practicality. A new wing was added to Middlesbrough High School and, said the *Gazette*, "the streets wore an animated appearance". At the same time, tea was provided for 700 paupers, and the "inmates of the workhouse found food aplenty this morning".

On December 28, 1897, came the news of "a terrible disaster in Scotland" . . . and its shadow hung over the whole of Teesside. It was the horror of the Tay Bridge collapse in a storm and a whole train plunged into the river below with dreadful loss of life. "The vast construction had emanated from the Tees Engine Works, Middlesbrough", the *Gazette* informed its readers. A measure of blame was later to be laid on that company, which was also faithfully chronicled.

The Nineties opened with the first-ever football edition of the *Gazette*. It reported that Middlesbrough F.C. had beaten Mossend Swifts 5-1. The decade ended in sorrow as the Boer War guns boomed in earnest.

In the autumn of 1898, the lull before the storm, Middlesbrough proudly boasted its maturity with a grand Trades and Arts Exhibition "within the spacious buildings that now cover Victoria Square".

The *Gazette*, of course, was on the spot with a display all its own. On the same day there were warnings of the Chinese peril, the urgent need for a lighthouse at Saltburn and the arrest of a Malton parson for poaching.

So the troubled century drew to a close, strife raging in South Africa, Mafeking relieved, Ladysmith relieved, Transvaal annexed, Parliament dissolved, Australia declared a Commonwealth . . . and the *Gazette* faithfully recorded the history, so often with a local reflection because somehow Teessiders seemed to be at the heart of it. As the Boer War opened with a clang, the *Gazette* was in jingoistic mood with a headline: "Loftus youth shoots six before breakfast".

Gordon is dead, Khartoum lost

Many die in Tay bridge disaster

Stockton High Street at the turn of the century

The New Century

TWENTY-TWO days after the century ended, Queen Victoria died. It was the end of an era. The dawn of the Twentieth Century began in mourning.

The *Gazette* moved into the new times making its own history. In 1906 the latest printing presses were acquired and installed both in the firm's head office in Middlesbrough and its district publishing office at Bishop Auckland.

The old gas plant was ripped out, and a modern electric power plant took over. The latest stereotyping machines went into the foundry, and all the time the Gazette's circulation was going up and up.

"The *Gazette* seems to be in the hands of every man, woman and child", wrote Lady Bell, wife of ironfounder, Sir Hugh Bell, when she conducted a survey into the reading habits of the steel workers in 1909.

The Bishop Auckland office had been opened on August 25, 1904, after it was found that many of the miners and iron workers in Auckland and the South West Durham area looked on the *Gazette* as a kind of working man's bible.

They were always ready to "stand or fall" by what the paper said, a conviction shared by the older people in the mining communities, the only folk left in these once-thriving townships and villages.

For many years the main feature pages were set in Middlesbrough and the matrix or casting mould was taken each morning by special messenger to the *Gazette* printing works in Cockton Hill Road, Bishop Auckland.

The messenger travelled by train or road according to the weather and the times of available public transport. It was a job of great responsibility for without these important pages the *Gazette* was incomplete, and during the winter months it frequently became a journey of considerable hazard.

The tiny staff team performed production and editorial wonders among the warm-hearted mining families in that somewhat disfigured part of Durham, and in later years, under the tutorship of Matt Winchester, it became a splendid training ground for budding young journalists.

The late Sir Denis Hamilton, one-time editor in chief of Times Newspapers, and a former editor of *The Sunday Times,* did his stint as a *Gazette* relief sub-editor at Cockton Hill Road. Sir Denis, perhaps the *Gazette's* most famous "old boy", joined the editorial staff direct from school to be given a training in the arts of journalism that he later described as "pure gold".

During the dark days of depression in Bishop Auckland after the First World War, at least 30 pits were either closed or abandoned within only a year or two and unemployment in the colliery towns and villages averaged between 70 and 80 per cent — even 100 per cent in some isolated communities dependent on one small local pit. The *Gazette* struggled to maintain publication in South West Durham, for it was the miners' main communication with the outside world.

Times were harsh for the hard-up miners and their families and the *Gazette* was the popular medium through which they were kept informed and could use as a public forum to express their dire needs. It was a local platform, too, for both union leaders, management and government to air their particular opinions and the professionalism of the *Gazette's* reporting and its integrity were again praised by all sides in a fraught situation.

The Bishop Auckland office remained in use until the *Gazette's* new modern premises in Borough Road were completed in 1938, when faster production methods and transport made separate printing presses unnecessary.

On November 6, 1911, with circulation records being broken weekly and profits increasing almost monthly, the *Gazette* recorded with sadness the sudden passing of its celebrated founder, Sir Hugh Gilzean Reid, who had a heart attack at Tenterden Hall in Middlesex, at the age of 73. Such was the affection and respect of the whole of Teesside that for three days the paper went into deep mourning, with thick obituary-black lines printed between each column.

By any yardstick, Gilzean Reid was a man touched by greatness. His influence on the growth of the embryo Teesside was as marked as was the success of the *Gazette* itself. His frankness, kindness, honesty, fairness, reforming zeal and outspoken support for human rights and the dignity of man, at a period when people frequently came second to the interests of industry and industrialists, gave the readers a sense of social justice that they would otherwise not have had, and was certainly wanting in other similar towns.

Apart from a set back in a newspaper consortium backed by Andrew Carnegie, the Scots-American steel baron, and Samuel Storey, the Sunderland newspaper proprietor and M.P., which was largely in promotion of the Liberal cause, Hugh Gilzean Reid had known only hard work and success since he entered journalism. His talents were wide-ranging and because he was a consummate organiser of himself as well as his businesses, he put them all to valuable use. Among his unexpected accomplishments, he was a pioneer of the co-operative house-building movement, helping thousands of working men to buy their own homes. He set out his ideas in a book that created much controversy at the time, yet he also proved himself a successful novelist with Old Oscar, which sold half-a-million copies and was translated into several languages.

He wrote deeply-thoughtful biographies of President Garfield and artist Jacob Thompson, with all the detailed images and impressions that the journalist in him had been storing away for years, as well as at least half-a-dozen works on his beloved Scotland. He found time, as the Who's Who of 1898 put it, to take "an aggressive part in helping, explaining, and defending King Leopold's scheme of colonial expansion in the Congo Free State".

His political career as Liberal member for Aston Moor lasted only a year and ended in 1886, but even here he left his mark as he was a prime mover in the establishment of the International Penny Post.

It was fittingly for his services to journalism that he received his knighthood in 1893, but by then he was recognised around the world as the epitome of a successful businessman with interests in publishing, and a major share holder in local steel and iron companies.

Gilzean Reid always said he had three great passions in his life — his native Scotland, the *Gazette* and his adopted Teesside, which he came to love and call home. It was understandable that he chose Middlesbrough as his last resting place, which he had helped to shape in what turned out to be his life's work.

Escape from Northallerton Gaol

The police have not succeeded in capturing the man Martin, who escaped from Northallerton gaol on Friday week. They have, however, recognised his clothes, from his sister's house, where he had gone and changed his clothes.

— 1889

The Great War

IT WAS just as well Gilzean Reid had left his newspaper in such a strong position and with firm hands at the helm like David Craig's. The signals of impending European conflict were there for all to see and the calamity of the Great War struck in 1914. Like the rest of Teesside, staff members donned uniform and marched off to battle. Despite a chronic shortage of newsprint and manpower, editor William Robertson brought the *Gazette* out every day with the news from the war fronts, and even managed a special edition on Sundays to keep Teesside informed of the latest turn of events.

War also commandeered the home news, and Teessiders applauded when a *Gazette* headline declared that the German ship Minotas had been seized "in the King's name" at Dent's Wharf, Middlesbrough. Even a royal visit to the area passed with only the merest mention, for the movements of the King and Queen were a closely-guarded state secret. As Stockton became increasingly concerned over food supplies, suddenly the full horror of war struck the North-east with frightening reality. A German battleship bombarded the Hartlepools, Whitby and Scarborough causing "scenes of death and destruction" and the whole of England feared further brazen attacks on her coastline industrial towns. In November 1916 Zeppelins launched a major bombing attack resulting in "great fires", reported a German newspaper. "But," said the *Gazette,* "it was the usual distortion of the truth".

As the lists of dead and wounded lengthened in the *Gazette* columns, so the anti-German feeling mounted. Even the letters to the editor column was full of the asides of war, the pathetic, the humorous, the angry, especially over the bane of everyone's existence, the black-out. P.C. Kilgannon, the first Stockton policeman to make a charge under the black-out order, also filed the last charge of the war, but the Armistice foiled him from recording yet another notch to his truncheon, for the bunting and flags were out, as well as "other symbols of rejoicing betokening the day of deliverance from the German yoke", and the case was dismissed.

As Europe began the great clean-up after the holocaust, the *Gazette* was ready to point the road for the future: "Give the League of Nations a fair chance", it urged, "the Allied countries must get rid of their jingo ministries. The new times call for men of democratic sympathies".

With the shouts of victory still ringing, the *Gazette* held its own celebrations in 1919 for its Jubilee, the year H.W. Le Prevost was appointed editor on demobilisation from the army. At a special dinner party the whole staff paid tribute to the now ageing David Craig, that favourite director and chairman who had done so much to establish the paper. They presented him with a beautifully-carved and illuminated Address that made the old man's eyes glisten. For him the words conjured the memories of 40 years:

> *"The North-Eastern Daily Gazette celebrates its Jubilee during the current month. You assisted at its inception; you have controlled its later development. The happy lot of devoting half a century to a task so useful falls to few men; amongst those few seldom is the high opportunity so honourably employed.*

"In the influence for good, at once moderate and inspiring which the Gazette wields over a wide area, the public pay their tribute to your eminent services. A very good cause has in you a steadfast friend; every abuse an unflinching enemy . . ."

Then general manager Arthur Pickering prophesied even further success for the paper. "We enter our second half century", he said, "with the hope that at the end of it the progress achieved will far exceed the marvellous development of the past". Arthur Pickering, cautious as always, never committed himself to a forecast that had a chance of failure, and as he spoke he knew with satisfaction that those successes were assured.

And because the *Gazette* is a family affair, Mr Richard Grunwell, J.P., whose memory of the newspaper reached back beyond that of any other employee, spoke up for the fair treatment of the staff. "There are 16 of us here", he said, "who can boast an aggregate of 500 years' service, and 35 others who have 20 to 44 years' service. You can be sure they wouldn't have stayed all this time if they did not like it", he added with a chuckle. Had Mr Grunwell been able to look forward as well as he could look back, he would have seen his own family carry on the tradition. His grandson, Robert Grunwell, not even born at the time, was to be chief sub-editor of the *Gazette* when the paper reached its century and later assistant editor and editor of the Chester Chronicle. His brother Fred was also a long-serving member of the sub-editor's desk.

All the while, behind the scenes and over the years, Arthur Pickering had been waging a private war with the Post Office. Towards the middle of 1922, he held a victory celebration of his own. With the help of Mr. G.B. Hodgson, a former member of the *Gazette* staff who became editor and manager of the *Shields Gazette*, and Sir Meredith Whitaker, proprietor of the *Scarborough Evening News*, it was finally agreed that direct lines could be installed in their respective offices permitting the use of Creed news receiving machines.

It meant the end of the era of the old rice-paper flimsies, those familiar buff coloured telegram forms that had seen service for years, bringing news of the world hotpacing from London. But now — instant news! News flashed across the country at tremendous speed to whole chains of newspapers simultaneously, providing an unparalleled service to readers of national and world events within minutes of them happening.

With such a sophisticated service added to the already strong local coverage, the *Gazette* took even further strides in circulation, consolidating in the far-flung areas, then pushing still further ahead, especially in Auckland and South Durham.

It was significant that readers in these two areas, geographically not even in *Gazette* territory, but nonetheless loyal and staunch followers because they appreciated reliable and accurate reporting, should turn to the paper in ever increasing numbers.

Soon the *Gazette* was to play a leading role in their lives. With Europe in tatters after the carnage of the Great War, our Land Fit for Heroes, where hardly a family remained unscathed, was exhausted.

As the first ecstasy of peace faded, fat dark clouds began to muster on the industrial front, growing increasingly ominous. The dole queues lengthened, the voices of the workers were raised, first in question and alarm, then depression and anguish, finally in anger.

British soldiers at the battle of the Somme, 1916

Strike!

THE General Strike came in 1926, with rumours that newspapers were likely to be swept up in the mass closures. Arthur Pickering, who at that time was also chairman of the Press Association, dashed back from London by car. On that first day, May 14, a one-sheet *Gazette* rolled from the presses with the following notice: "The *Gazette* will continue to appear in order that the public of North Yorkshire and South Durham may be kept in close and constant touch with the developments of the great economic and social crisis in both its national and local aspects".

The *Gazette* tells its own story of those tense days.

"**May 4**: Every endeavour is being made to maintain the gas supply, but the quantity of coal is limited, and as stocks cannot now be replenished, consumers are strongly urged to restrict the use of gas for all purposes while the trouble lasts.

"**May 5**: the Middlesbrough Transporter Bridge service will cease to operate from midnight.

"**May 7**: The first outbreak of rioting on a serious scale occurred in Middlesbrough last night and ugly scenes occurred before order was eventually restored at a late hour.

"It appeared that the last train had passed the distant signal from Thornaby, and an attempt was made by the stationmaster, Mr. Walker, to close the gates of the Sussex Street level crossing. A very large crowd had assembled and there was much booing and cheering at the stationmaster's failure to close the gates.

"The police were telephoned for and on arrival they found that the crowd were preventing the gates from being closed. Increasing in numbers, the crowd swayed to and fro and eventually rushed the gates and swarmed onto the railway lines towards Thornaby.

"The Constabulary were in fairly good strength assisting the railway police to try to clear the lines. Unfortunately, Chief Inspector Heald and Inspector Bentley were driven into a cul-de-sac and stoned by the crowd. They were obliged to draw their batons to force the crowd back — Chief Inspector Heald and Sgt Winter being somewhat seriously hurt at this time.

"One portion of the crowd — mainly youths — attempted to overturn a bus at Queen's Square and the police were stoned when they arrested a youth. There were further attacks on the goods station.

"The Mayor (Councillor W.H. Crosthwaite) and Councillor T. Meehan exhorted the crowd outside the town hall not to commit any acts of violence and to disperse quietly to their own homes. A very pleasing feature at the end of the occurrence was that the crowd accepted the advice of the two gentlemen referred to."

With two destroyers, the Wakefield and the Whirlwind, stationed in the Tees as watchdogs, the *Gazette* did its best to keep the public informed and play its own part in cooling trouble with sane comment. The paper received much praise from all quarters, especially in Auckland and South Durham, where the miners and their families were undergoing the most severe hardship.

Volunteer women mail drivers took over deliveries during the strike.

In an attempt to relieve some of the suffering, the *Gazette* set about organising and distributing gifts of boots, shoes and clothing, and there were many letters of appreciation and gratitude for little acts of kindness that most people knew nothing about.

In the best traditions of a community newspaper, the *Gazette* brought help where it was needed most — to the families at risk in the the mining heartland of Auckland and South Durham. At the same time, the *Gazette's* factual and unbiased reporting of the strike won the newspaper respect and many friends. It may have been seen to support the miners' families, but journalistically it was accurate, professional and independent.

A New Owner

AS the National Strike ended, the whole country still reeling, the *Gazette* suddenly made its own headlines. At last Mr. Craig had sought his well-earned retirement, and it was announced on August 10, 1926, that the *North-Eastern Daily Gazette* had been taken over by Allied Newspapers Ltd, under the chairmanship of Mr. Edward Tebbutt.

There was immediate speculation by staff and public over what was to happen to their beloved newspaper, for it was the first time the *Gazette* had changed hands since Sir Hugh launched it, and the prospect of a new management was viewed with suspicion.

In fact, there was no cause for concern. Allied Newspapers was the group owned by the remarkable Berry brothers, better known in later years as Lord Camrose and Lord Kemsley, who startled the Press world by the sheer speed of their dramatic emergence from obscurity to become newspaper magnates and peers of the realm.

In 1915 they had acquired the long-established *Sunday Times*, already having in their possession a number of small journals. It was the start of their race to fame. In quick succession the onslaught began by taking into the Berry fold the *Financial Times*, the *St. Clements Press*, the *Graphic* group, Cassels, Kelly's Directories, and Weldons Ltd.

Soon the Kemsley empire extended throughout the country, with newspapers in Aberdeen, Glasgow, Newcastle, Middlesbrough, York, Blackburn, Manchester, Stockport, Sheffield, Macclesfield, Cardiff and London.

The group became famous for its enlightened approach to newspaper production and each paper was carefully briefed in the Kemsley doctrine.

"A newspaper must present the news, both local and national, with the highest degree of accuracy, both in presentation and in balance", Viscount Kemsley once said. "It must provide instruction and entertainment for its readers according to its tastes.

"Finally, it must make comment and express opinion on the events of the day, whether they be of local or of national interest, and this duty, performed as fearlessly as it is performed honestly, endows the paper with its character and individuality. This is the policy which guides us. Each of our provincial papers has a character of its own determined by and suited to the locality in which it circulates."

The Kemsley philosophy certainly brought advances. But to keep the continuity of the already successful *Gazette* policy intact, Arthur Pickering became a director and eventually succeeded the brilliant Edward Tebbutt as chairman. Mr. Tebbutt, who died in 1934 at the age of 56, had become a director of Allied Newspapers in charge of the Manchester organisation as well as the Newcastle Chronicle Ltd.

By this time, of course, the changes, improvements and developments had been continuing on the *Gazette*. In common with almost all the other newspapers, the price of the *Gazette* had been increased from the magical halfpenny to a penny. Indeed, in 1920 it had even jumped to threehalfpence, although in the following year it was again reduced to a penny. It was clear, however, even then, that the days of the cheap Press were numbered.

In 1927 the redoubtable J. H. Thompson

Stockton High Street, 1929

succeeded Mr. W. Le Prevost as editor, and continued in the chair for an amazing 21 years.

Born and bred in Middlesbrough, and at one time or another occupying every editorial post on the *Gazette* on his way to the editorship, Jack Thompson dedicated his life to championing the causes which were for the good of Teesside, the area to which he was devoted. Because iron and steel were the lifeblood of Teesside at the time, Jack made himself an authority on the subjects.

On one occasion when an ill-informed M.P. stood up in the House of Commons and declared that Teesside's steel trade was declining, Jack took up his pen in fierce reprisal — and there were few leader writers as fearless as Jack Thompson — and by facts and figures and devastating argument in fine literary style reduced the Honourable Member to apology. Arthur Pickering and a number of prominent people in the steel trade were so impressed by the argument that they immediately booked space in The

Times for the following day, and the article was reproduced in full. It caused immense satisfaction on Teesside, and there were many letters of praise and pint glasses raised in a toast to the editor of the *Gazette.*

Always ready to try out new ideas, big Jack became an evening newspaper pioneer in 1928 by replacing advertisements on page one with news. Such a revolutionary step caused considerable controversy, but Jack Thompson's thinking was frequently ahead of his times, and he had the courage to force his ideas into the paper.

Mr. Thompson came from a family of journalists. His son and daughter were on the *Gazette,* and two of his brothers, Harry, who was killed in the First World War, and Ernie, also worked on the editorial staff. When the lanky Ernie Thompson retired in 1967, he was assistant sports editor, and he and Jack between them had served the *Gazette* for 98 years.

On the Move

URING all this time, of course, Middlesbrough had been growing, stretching out a beckoning arm to the villages along its boundaries, and the *Evening Gazette* expanded with it. The increasing space requirements of a fast-moving evening newspaper demanded more than its old home in Zetland Road could offer, and the decision had to be taken to move.

The very nature of a newspaper makes its position in relation to the town's main activities of vital importance. It must have ready access to the law courts, the town council, hospitals, fire station, police, railways and other services at the town's heart, yet it must also be so positioned that clogging traffic does not impede distribution in those ubiquitous *Gazette* vans. The site at the junction of Woodlands Road and Borough Road, where the old Middlesbrough vicarage once stood, seemed to have all the essentials.

In Middlesbrough the scars of the iron revolution were still too vivid to give the town any kind of architectural pride or heritage. So when the time arrived, in the mid 1930s, to decide on the shape and appearance of the new *Evening Gazette* building, it would have been easy to conform to the surrounding Coronation Street theme then prevalent in the centre of the town.

No one would have complained or even been surprised if the new building had been created in the stark and functional architectural culture of a factory. It is to the enduring credit of the management of the *Evening Gazette* that they built with dignity and grace and elegance in fine Portland

stone to create one of the most pleasing and architecturally-interesting buildings in Teesside.

But what a job in changing house! A removal at the best of times is a complicated affair, but the problems of moving a whole newspaper, lock, stock and newsprint, are enough to make an editor tear his hair. And because one of the adages in journalism is that the paper must come out, it meant that the complete operation had to be carried through without a break in publication.

Just imagine that daunting task. Dismantling machines while the operators were still tapping keyboards, reporters chasing stories, photographers flashing cameras, sub-editors scribbling headlines and flourishing glue-pots with an eye on the clock, the Creed telegraphic machines chattering, advertising men selling space, the presses rumbling, the maroon vans fast delivering. To move in the middle of that bedlam was a nightmare!

The planning started well in advance. For two weeks there had been a steady flow of all sorts of goods and chattels to the new building. Books, back numbers, old files, commercial records and all the papers common to large offices were speeded along. As joiners erected new shelves and racks, so they were quickly filled up. Stocks of paper and ink had to be laid in. It was necessary to have at least 150 tons of newsprint ready in those giant reels, each weighing almost three-quarters of a ton and containing four miles of paper.

Two weeks before zero hour, squads of engineers began to dismantle what printing machinery could be spared and transported to Borough Road in a fleet of lorries, and

Kemsley House building, completed 1938

even a horse and cart. The position of each new machine had been carefully planned, and electricians and plumbers had supplies of electricity, gas and water all ready to connect up.

For the removal of those heavy and intricate linotype machines, six skilled mechanics came specially to Middlesbrough, each with two labourers to assist him. Each machine weighed nearly a ton and it required knocking out the windows on two floors plus specially-built lifting tackle to winch them the 70 feet down into Zetland Road below. The work went on through Saturday night, heaving, grunting, pushing, lowering with bated breath, one ear cocked for the crash that never came, then rushing them over to Borough Road, where that small force of commando mechanics threw themselves upon the machines, tinkering, cajoling, willing that familiar clickety-clack metallic

language to ring out as fluently as ever by Monday morning. While this activity was reaching crescendo, the photographers had been hurrying along the pictures for Saturday's paper, and the picture process crew worked deep into the Friday night to make the blocks. Almost before the last one had been completed, the process and photographic departments had vanished, whisked away with all their paraphernalia to the new building to be quickly reconnected ready for use. And all the time, edition after edition, the *Evening Gazette* presses were thundering out the news of the day:

"Big Laundry Fire, Murdered Pyjama Girl, Boro's Ralph Birkett transferred to Newcastle, Gliders collide in mid-air, Heatwave Heroics, Nazi Chief on right to colonise, Threat of trouble in Jamaica."

North-Eastern Gazette

ESTABLISHED 1869.   MIDDLESBROUGH, FRIDAY, AUGUST 16, 1940.   THREE-HALFPENCE

Previous Record Doubled By The R.A.F.

169 NAZIS DOWN YESTERDAY

1,000 Raiders Over Front Of 500 Miles

OF THE 1,000 German bombers and fighters attacking our shores on a 500-mile front from Plymouth to the Tyne yesterday, 169 are now known to have been destroyed. The R.A.F. wrote a new page of glory.

The R.A.F.'s previous best "bag" was 78. Of the 169 destroyed yesterday, 153 were shot down by fighters, 11 by A.A., one by Lewis gun and two by infantry fire.

Thirty-four of our 'planes were lost, but the pilots of 17 are safe. And to-day the toll of enemy machines continues.

One Nazi bomber was shot down by our fighters in the Humber area in the early hours to-day, while this afternoon at least one enemy bomber was destroyed when 16 raided a South-East England town. Bombs were dropped but no-one was killed. Another Nazi 'plane also fell in South-East England.

Exclusive of to-day's "bag," Germany in five days has lost 406 'planes and a total of 807 brought down in and around Britain since the war began.

But enemy 'planes also attacked areas on the North-East Coast of England, where one was seen in the beam of searchlights to fall to destruction, and a district in South-East England, while they were reported at various times over the North-West Coast of England, the South-West and also Wales.

Raiders visited one town four times, most of the bombs dropped falling on open country. Three horses were killed.

On the North-East coast the raid was one of the biggest yet experienced, though lone 'planes are thought to have been responsible.

In one district six loud explosions were followed by a huge red glare, and as more 'planes approached from the sea every type of land defence was brought into action, despite which some more bombs were heard.

R.A.F. In Near East

Libyan Seaplane Base Bombed

YESTERDAY'S R.A.F. communique from Cairo states:—
Highly successful raid was carried out on Bomba (Libya) by aircraft of the R.A.F. yesterday... ...causing damage on a number of flying boat aircraft in the harbour. ...started fire was started... ...ignited the flying-boat base and two flying-boats.

THE REMAINS of a German aeroplane brought down in flames in the North-East during the large-scale air raid.

Nazis Lose More Than A Week's 'Plane Output

Somaliland Situation Critical

The situation in Somaliland is now regarded as rather critical. It looks as if the British forces there may have to fall back on Berbera.

There are two Italian divisions...

Moyale Garrison Daring Escape

JOHANNESBURG, Fri

IT WAS ONLY after they been bombed and shelled after day for a month by superior Italian forces that the officers and men holding Moyale on the Kenya frontier decided to withdraw from the...

The story of their withdrawal on the night of July 14 was to-day by an official eye-witness Kenya of the Union Government Bureau of Information.

He said: "Lieutenant in the Union, but who is no officer in the King's African told me how the Italians eventually surrounded the tiny, towered fort and held up the relief force marching to the besieged garrison.

"With the water supply fort running low and the site of the defenders becoming serious the officers, including Dutoit, and the N.C.O.s agreed a plan to evacuate.

"The spirit of the men magnificent," he said, were all determined no surrender."

CREPT THROUGH LINE

Early in the evening of July Lieut. Dutoit crept out of fort and cut a path through rows of double-barbed wire.

The 200 officers and men...

War and Peace

THE dark shadows of war were gathering again. The *Gazette* had sounded the warnings: the uncertain Thirties, the rise of Hitler, the threat of Hitler, the race to arms, and the world tensing for the onslaught. Then the false relief when at the eleventh hour disaster seemed incredibly averted. On September 30, 1938, the *Gazette* screamed the betrayed hope in a banner headline: " 'No More War' Pact Signed Between Britain and Germany", and the message from the Prime Minister under the quotation "Peace in our Time", which said, "I had always had in mind that if we could find a peaceful solution of this problem of Czechoslovakia we should open the way to general appeasement of Europe. This morning I talked with the Fuehrer. We both signed the following declaration: 'We, the German Fuehrer and Chancellor, and the British Prime Minister, have had a further meeting today and are agreed in recognising that the question of Anglo-German relations is of the first importance for the two countries and for Europe.

'We regard the agreement signed last night and the Anglo-German Naval Agreement as symbolic of the desire of our two peoples never to go to war with one another again . . .' "

And as "Mr Neville Chamberlain the Peacemaker returned home to a tumultuous welcome", a front page editorial by the editor commented: "Hour by hour, minute by minute, news and rumour have changed their face. Restraint has been called for. We venture to believe that this restraint has been observed. This paper has endeavoured to steer a calm and clear course without exaggeration, extravagance or sensationalism. Hysteria and sabre-rattling have had no place in these columns. In almost every leading article during the past ten days we have urged our leaders to trust the Prime Minister. How far we have been justified in that hope we leave you to judge. Peace is here."

A year later that scrap of paper that had carried the tremulous hopes of Europe was forgotten. Hope sometimes blinds men to the ugliness of truth, and Neville Chamberlain and the *Evening Gazette* were in a fine and vast company of those who had been proved wrong.

On September 3, 1939, with silent little gatherings clustered around every available wireless set, came the solemn and momentous announcement: "Britain is now at a state of war with Germany..."

Mr George Pratt, who had been appointed manager in April, 1938, heard the news and surveyed the *Gazette's* fine new building, and all its costly modern machinery and the men who operated it and contemplated the headlines that blared the holocaust to come. He sighed and instructed

that the major part of the composing equipment should be moved into the basement, hopefully safe from bombs and blasts.

The little team bent their backs to it on a Saturday night after the last edition. There were seven labourers, four electricians, the linotype engineer and the works manager. They had to shift 26 machines, weighing about a ton each, seven composing stones with a total weight of three tons, and all the stereotype equipment.

Two of the biggest linotypes had to be stripped before they could be moved at all. Dismantling would take three hours at least, and another three hours to reassemble them. The smaller machines fitted into the lift with about half an inch to spare. Some of them had to be manhandled about 50 yards to the lift, and another 50 yards to their new position in the basement. Even as the men were struggling with one of the larger machines on the Sunday, the air raid sirens were wailing over Middlesbrough. The works manager ran up on to the roof to act as spotter, and the toil went on.

Around 100 tons of paper had to be moved out of the basement, and most of it went into the lino room as the machines were taken out. The lift was not accustomed to these loads, and troubles came, the main one being a tendency to overshoot the basement floor. The first time this happened, one of the men had to wind the lift into position by hand. It was then decided to use the emergency stop, the works manager proving himself the most skilful at this game, being less than a couple of inches out. The electricians used nearly a thousand yards of new wire to connect the machines in their new positions. And on Monday morning they were chattering

---

Krupps' Essen Works bombed by RAF

Bombers of the RAF attacked targets at Essen, Bremen and Bremerhaven last night, while Britain was raid free for the second night in succession. No bombs have been dropped on the country for 48 hours.

June 4, 1941

Luftwaffe Unable to Dominate the Skies

1941

away as usual in their wartime bunker as if it was their permanent home, recording the events of a world suddenly plunged into turmoil.

On September 4, 1939, the day after war was declared, the *Gazette* reported: "Intense but orderly activity in Middlesbrough official circles followed the announcement on Saturday night that the town was to be evacuated of children according to the scheme that had been submitted to London. Most parents were delighted that the evacuation was scheduled to begin virtually at once, even though the eventual destination of their children was unknown last night".

On September 6, the *Gazette* announced that "residents in Middlesbrough will welcome the news that the local authorities have earmarked certain big basements in the town for use, day and night, as shelters against air attacks, for those who may be caught in the streets".

The evacuees poured into East Cleveland and beyond, shelters were dug in back gardens all over Teesside, League football was suspended, petrol was rationed, gas masks fitted, sandbags filled, identity cards issued, and while Charlie Kunz tried to bring a little cheer at the Middlesbrough Empire the *Gazette,* with Nelson-like patriotism, reminded its readers that "England expects that every man this day will do his duty".

The *Gazette* did its duty by adhering to strict economy measures, which meant a reduction in size and paging, as well as a change of title. A page one explanation said that "the war has speeded up the tempo of our lives. Gone are the leisurely days and ways of peace. In every phase of industrial effort, the emphasis is upon speed and the elimination of the unessential.

"In tune with this universal acceleration, the title of *The North-Eastern* *Gazette* is today altered to the *Evening Gazette.*

"Limitations of the size of newspapers has dictated the practice of condensation and the abbreviation of the title is in conformity with that trend. As heretofore, it will still be our aim to present the news — all the news — without bias."

Although Press censorship would not allow the publication of the specific areas where the bombs fell, Teessiders knew well enough what that cryptic phrase "a densely populated area in the North-east" meant. During those dark days the people kept morale high with light-hearted optimism, even on the days of gloomiest news, while no chance was lost to destroy the image of Hitler's strength. After one particularly heavy raid the *Gazette* was delighted to point out that "the only casualties were two canaries".

Those who came through those fearful days will never forget the frenzy with which each copy of the *Gazette* was read, again and again. Britain was fighting for its survival, every citizen was involved, and the *Gazette* was recording the grim struggle blow by blow.

"Fury of the Battle of France", screamed the headlines. "Bravery of the Guards, R.A.F.'s V.C.s bomb vital bridge, Fanatical Nazi Pilots, Air fight at 50 feet".

As the war progressed, gradually the headlines began to reflect the changing tides, then the full flood to victory. "Monty has 'em on the Run, Prisoners By the Acre, Rome Falls, Invasion!, Hitler is Dead, Germany Surrenders" shouted the Gazette as the Allies fought their way across Europe.

May 10, 1945, saw Mayor Kitching touring Middlesbrough on V.E. night, with the crowds cheering, the streets decorated, and the *Gazette* reporting that "Teessiders celebrated with accustomed good spirits", music in the streets of Stockton, free beer in West Hartlepool and revelry so noisy in Stilesley that magistrates had to delay court proceedings.

On August 15, the *Gazette* was reporting "a large crowd outside the Middlesbrough municipal buildings, when the mayor formally announced the end of hostilities with Japan.

"The jubilation on Teesside on receipt of the news of the Japanese surrender found expression in numerous ways. The feelings

---

Boro Star Shines Again in Army Soccer Duel

Following his superb display in the British Army team in Belfast, Wilf Mannion, the Middlesbrough F.C. inside right, captivated the Scottish crowd at Dumfries, when he starred in another service victory, this time against a Scottish eleven.

During the second half the South Bank lad made a great solo run — practically the length of the field — which almost brought a goal. The former Middlesbrough right-winger, Ralph Birkett, scored the winning goal for the Army eleven which ended in a 2-1 Khaki victory

1941

WAR . . . and the Army is on the move

of the people were such that they were unable to await tonight's official bonfires.

"They hastily accumulated all manner of combustible material, including some household articles which ought never to have been burned at street corners, and pranced round flames until 2 am and 3 am."

Peace on Teesside brought the Max Lock plan for Middlesbrough, "a challenge to the social conscience of the community", as the *Gazette* put it. Peace brought a general election with the *Gazette* predictably campaigning for the Conservatives — it's "either Churchill for a free, happier and greater Britain . . . or the whims of an obscure Socialist". Labour, as events proved,

were successful. Harold Macmillan was defeated in Stockton. The *Gazette* "awaited prompt evidence of the new government's readiness to substitute deeds for words". To the *Gazette* the founding of the United Nations was "the labour of practical idealists", but it was almost lost for words when Middlesbrough Football Club fought their way to the last eight in the 1946–47 F.A. Cup, the furthest the Boro had ever reached, for although they had won a place in the quarter finals on three other occasions, this game went into extra time. There was, of course, no scarcity of comment when Burnley eventually beat them 1–2, after a much-disputed goal.

Time to clear up after a night of terror on July 25, 1942.

Up the Boro

IN AN area like the North-east where every other man is an authority on football and racing (and beer for that matter) Teessiders are arguably the most knowledgeable, dedicated and demanding of sports followers. Their conversation is of football, of golden days past and present, wondrous goals, flying wingers, acrobatic 'keepers, poetic midfielders and of balmy days in the old Division One. And because the Boro is one of the most fickle teams in any division, also days of black despair. Or else the talk is of horses; pounds lost, shillings won, fortunes only a dream away. And remembering Teesside has produced some of the best swimmers, cyclists, boxers, athletes and even bowlers in Britain, it is hardly surprising readers of the *Evening Gazette* should expect — indeed insist — on the highest standards of sporting journalism.

Old Bird was first to recognise the fact. Old Bird who, as sports editor at the turn of the century, understood the craving by Teessiders for news and discussion on matters sporting — and he was determined to do something about it.

Old Bird was the pen-name of W. J. Gill, a tall, sartorially splendid man, who brought a little fragrance to the office each summer morning with a freshly-cut flower in his buttonhole, stuck there pristine from the garden by a doting Mrs Gill.

No one knew the area and its interests better than Jim Gill or could analyse more objectively the changing needs and patterns of sports reporting. In all this he was in advance of his times, for in the *Evening Gazette's* beginning days there was little sports coverage at all, except for the racing results. In fact, the very first

mention in the paper of any other sporting activity was the description of a Tees boat race, when Mr J. Nicholson, of Stockton, lifted the £20 prize by an emphatic 20 lengths.

Slowly, Jim Gill began to heighten the sports interest and quality, and the readers came with him. As they began to pressure him to produce more and more sporting news and information on a widening platform, he suddenly realised the urgent need to break with newspaper tradition. Although the next logical step was not at first obvious, journalistic instinct told him that he was on the threshhold of something major and he began to grope towards it. He took into his deliberations the burst of Saturday sport, the increasing week-end leisure time, the louder jingle in the public's pocket and, like a present-day marketing operation, he came to the conclusion there was only one satisfactory course open. The time was ripe to launch a quite separate *Sports Gazette* for Saturday evenings — and he must do it.

He knew what it would contain. All the latest sport and racing results, news of as many other sporting events as the paper could muster, full descriptions of matches played, debate and discussion, a soapbox for readers' views, a form guide for the following week, and behind-the-scenes gossip. And to spice the new paper with a sprinkling of controversy he would write some pungent sports comment himself, striking at the sporting anomalies of the day, fair and honest, in keeping with the policies of the paper, but so hard hitting and provocative that it simply could not be overlooked by the Teesside sporting fraternity.

Such a concept at that period was extraordinary. It was a bold and imaginative step and a pioneering one, for after it had been proved an outstanding success, other newspapers throughout the country began to copy the formula.

Printed on green paper, the *Sports Gazette* was an immediate rage. Swashbuckling Old Bird commanded instant respect and later affection and found an acclaim that reached far outside the North-east. It was he who launched the long-continuing campaign for the improvement of the game and football facilities and to promote sportsmanship, which have echoes to this day, and were taken up by other newspapers throughout Britain. Looking back across the years the result of the *Evening Gazette's* leadership in those distant days is astonishing.

One of Old Bird's understudies at the Bishop Auckland office was Robert Young, or Old Brahma as he was better known to the public in that age of journalists' nom-de-plumes. For the guidance of those who worked under him or came after, including such celebrities as the renowned Captain Jack and Cliff Mitchell, Bob Young set down his golden rule for would-be football writers. It is as valid today as it was then:

"Wield your pencil fairly, firmly, but never harshly. Remember, the pen can cut deeper than the sword."

This was the doctrine that brought acceptance and popularity. In all things, the *Evening Gazette* was straight, firm, outspoken, but always fair.

One of the proud traditions of the *Evening Gazette* sports department is the dedication with which the affairs of Middlesbrough F.C. have been recorded over the years. It is not an easy task, made more difficult by the Boro's capricious form that has continued for almost as long as any one can remember. Nothing gives the sports editor and his staff greater pleasure than to rejoice over a Boro triumph, but it is also the paper's task to report the good and the bad times and make judgements. It is an obligation taken seriously and the provision of a fair and accurate reflection of the team week by week throughout the season demands a grasp and insight into the workings of the club, the players, the policies as well as the backroom whispers that must rival the knowledge of the team manager himself.

Fortunately, the *Evening Gazette* has always had men of calibre to follow the Boro's fortunes. Before the last war Colin Reid, Will Grunwell (Erimus), Eddie Rose and then Jack Bavin, the illustrious Captain Jack, trailed the Boro through the First Division, at the same time as the famous David Jack was manager, and the two Jacks made a striking partnership. Captain Jack lived soccer. The grey trilby and drooping cigarette stuck firmly to his lower lip were his familiar symbols in Press boxes throughout the country and he gained the respect of supporters and players wherever he went.

Jack was also an expert with a billiard cue, and it was often said that if the Boro forwards could score goals like Captain Jack could pot reds, they would win the League flag, and the Cup to go with it. Jack Bavin died in June, 1947, and his young assistant, Cliff Mitchell, took over for what was to be one of the longest and most distinguished reigns as the *Gazette's* Boro reporter. Cliff also became Sports Editor and even followed his team to the reverse side of the world to report a Boro close-season tour of Australia. Cliff Mitchell covered the affairs of the Boro with distinction for almost a quarter of a century, fated, of course, to record the Boro's heartbreaks as well as their nights of drama and magic. Apart from maintaining the great tradition of *Gazette* sports editors as a character in his own right, Cliff was acknowledged by his professional peers as a supreme run-of-play reporter, a natural on radio and one of the best-known figures in Teesside. As one wag of the day put it during a Royal visit to the area, "Who's that lady with the tiara standing next to Cliff Mitchell?"

Few will forget Cliff's — and every Boro supporter's — night of horror in 1966, when the club plunged into the wilderness of the Third Division in the final game of the season against Cardiff City, who also faced relegation if they lost.

"It was quite a night. It had eight goals, a hat-trick by the centre-half of the beaten team, two stupid penalties, nerves, mistakes and tremendous endeavour. The lot. Silence, frightened silence greeted Boro's goals. A deafening roar succeeded each

Cardiff success. At the end, Hallelujah rang out over the terraces, for the Welsh express their emotion in song — and the crowd had something to sing about. It knew its team would still be in the Second Division next year".

The Boro, of course, were not and Cliff Mitchell's emotional words were followed up on page one with the pictures of the whole Boro board of directors to indicate they were "the guilty men". The *Gazette's* action was, to say the least, a talking point. It was unlikely the board of directors were enchanted. But it was important that the *Gazette* spoke out truthfully and frankly, as it felt it had to do, on an issue of importance to the community, just as its founder had decreed almost a century before.

The increasing production pressures on the sports editor and his team of sub-editors inside the office made it impossible for Cliff to cover the affairs of the Boro and edit the sports pages simultaneously. So Cliff passed on the sports editorship and concentrated on his beloved team and was rewarded by watching Jackie Charlton take the Boro back where they belong — to the top drawer of English football with a runaway Second Division championship in 1974. The celebrations came to a crescendo in Borough Road as the team bus was forced to a standstill by a remarkable sight — it seemed as if the red-and-white horde of the Ayrsome Angels had deserted the terracing to gather outside the *Gazette* office to greet their conquering heroes in an ecstatic, heaving sea of red and white.

Or like those equally unforgettable scenes for a club starved of silverware as the red tide flowed down the motorway to a Wembley final in the Zenith Data Systems Cup in 1990 — only to lose narrowly 1-0 to Chelsea. But what an occasion! And what a hunger for more! Who will forget the titanic struggles with the big glamorous clubs like Arsenal and Manchester United and Liverpool in whose company the Boro have been on equal footing with the crowd stamping its feet in the main stand and chanting "Boro, Boro, Boro..." willing their team to a winning goal? Or the great names that have graced the turf from the distant days of Alf Common, Steve Bloomer, Ralph Birkett, George

Washington Elliott, the talented Carr brothers George and Jackie, George Camsell, Bobby Baxter, George Hardwick, the legendary Wilf Mannion, Mickey Fenton, Harold Sheperdson MBE, Roberto Ugolini, Lindy Delapenha, the prolific goal scorer Brian Clough, Nobby Stiles, John Hickton, Eric McMordie, Willie Maddren, Stuart Boam, Graeme Souness, Gary Pallister and a cast of hundreds more right up to the present time.

There have been so many memorable moments for the Boro recorded by Cliff Mitchell, his reporting successor Paul Daniel and now, in the *Gazette's* 125th year, by the respected Eric Paylor who, with the title of Deputy Sports Editor as well as Chief Sports Writer, indicates the importance the newspaper places on following the affairs of the Boro. Whatever the differences of how a game is separately viewed by football writers and football players they share a common cause. The *Gazette* team, the team on the park and the fans all seek the same elusive target — success. And the newspaper has even underlined its support by being the club's sponsor.

Of course, the *Gazette's* involvement with the Teesside sporting community has not revolved around football alone. The area has produced some of the finest sporting headlinemakers in the country — in some instances in the world — and the newspaper has taken great pleasure in sharing the fame and triumphs with its readers. Like cricketers Chris and Alan Old; rugby internationalists Rory and Tony Underwood and Rob Andrew; golfer Martin Thompson, the 1982 British Amateur champion; the 1986 Commonwealth Games cycling gold medallist Paul Curran; Mary Reveley, of Lingdale, the best woman horse trainer in the land and, over a century-and-a-quarter, a little army of Teesside sportsmen and sportswomen who have reached the highest flights in their respective fields.

Wilson League's top scorer
By Pathfinder

Each and all rendered a good account of himself, but to the defence must go a large share of the Teessider's laurels. Rarely has one witnessed the rear trio and the three halves so completely masters of the situation.

Boro: Harrison, Marshall, Fox, Davidson, Carr (W), Ellington, Carr (J), Birrell, Carr (G), Urwin, Wilson.

February 25, 1922

Jack Charlton is chaired shoulder high after Boro won the Second Division Championship in 1974.

But the sports desk, too, calls for particular talents. It is a very special area in a newspaper, almost like a paper within a newspaper, with its own editor, sports news and features writers, specialists, sub-editors and correspondents from around the world. The sports team must live the job and the occasion, succumb to the excitement of the moment, yet keep their cool and the journalists' necessary sense of perspective — and a loving dedication to the task. Teesside is an area also dedicated to the sporting cause and in this respect the *Gazette* and the sporting community have developed over the years almost hand-in-hand. Indeed, Middlesbrough Football Club is the *Gazette's*

younger brother by only seven years.

As the Gazette reaches its 125th birthday, the Boro moves away from its traditional stronghold of Ayresome Park to a new ground. It is a symbolic move. Inevitably, both events can be seen as the start of a new era for newspaper and club. It is a time to look ahead. What Boro stars and legends still-in-the-making — or even born — will emerge in the years to come? What swimmers, cyclists, climbers, cricketers, athletes, boxers, jockeys or trainers will be the celebrities of the future?

There is only one certainty — some dedicated scribe from the *Gazette's* sports desk will be there to record them.

Royal Teesside

ROYAL visits to the area have always brought out the crowds. Of course, when the *Gazette* was first published there were no photographs, but long reports recorded events in detail as word pictures. In the absence of cameras, sometimes drawings were produced like the one below marking the arrival of the Prince and Princess of Wales to Middlesbrough's "new" Town Hall in 1889.

In the following pages we record some of Teesside's Royal occasions, which also illustrate the improvements in cameras and processing.

To her Most Gracious Majesty Victoria, Queen of Great Britain and Ireland and Empress of India . . . began the scroll to the Queen from Middlesbrough in 1882 after her life had been endangered. The scroll went on: "May It Please Your Majesty, we, Your Majesty's most loyal and dutiful subjects, the Mayor, Aldermen and Burgesses of the Borough of Middlesbrough, in council assembled, venture to express to Your Majesty our deep abhorrence of the dastardly act by which the life of Your Majesty was recently placed in imminent peril, and to offer our most earnest and heartfelt congratulations on your Majesty's providential escape".

It was signed by Richard Archibald, Mayor, and Geo. Bainbridge, Town Clerk.

The scroll came to light in an antique shop in Kettering, Northamptonshire. The picture shows museums' assistant curator Richard Devaney, as it was placed in the Town Hall centenary exhibition in 1989.

The cover for the official programme of the Prince and Princess of Wales' visit on January 23, 1889. It may have been couched in the style of an age long gone, but it remains a good example of the high standards of design and printing of the day. Raylton Dixon was Mayor and the Town Clerk continued to be George Bainbridge.

Sailing up the Tees . . . King George V and Queen Mary visited munition works and shipyards as part of their country-wide tours to keep up spirits during the Great War. The year is 1917 and among the sites the Royal couple toured were Smith's Dock and the Harkess shipyard, situated between the Transporter Bridge and Dock Point in South Bank.

Let's have a party . . .and the street is the place to mark the Jubilee celebrations in Middlesbrough in May, 1935.

It is 1985 and a smiling Prince Charles and Princess Diana are given a right royal Teesside welcome at Middlesbrough railway station and throughout the whole of their visit to Cleveland.

Shake hands, Your Royal Highness! And Prince Charles is faced by a sea of outstretched arms as he visited the Enterprise Centre.

Royal Welcome

The happy Queen . . . as she opens the Hartlepool Marina in May 1993 and tours Teesside.

This plaque was unveiled
By
Her Royal Highness The Princess of
to commemorate the opening
of the
Cleveland Alzheimers Residential
on
September 23rd 1992

The weather may have been wet and cold, but it was "Sunshine Di", as the Gazette called her, on her visit to Teesside in September, 1992.

The pictures show her being greeted at the Alzheimer Centre and the official opening. She took time to talk to both staff and patients and even held some of their hands.

The Princess also called at South Cleveland Hospital to mark the 40th anniversary for Clinical Oncology Services in Cleveland and visit the refurbished Radiology and Oncology unit. It was smiles and laughs all the way for the caring Princess who seemed to make everyone feel better.

Flag day at Hartlepool . . . and the Queen responds with a big smile.

How do you do, Your Majesty? A guided visit to Stockton University by Vice Chancellor Professor Fraser.

The Duke of Edinburgh calls in for a chat at the sheltered housing development at Bramley Court, Hartlepool.

Mind your head, sir! The Duke stoops to navigate around HMS Tricomalee.

Making the *Gazette*

WELCOME to the hurly-burly world of the *Evening Gazette*. Life on an evening newspaper, edition by edition, is a frantic race against time. News is the raw material— and news won't wait. Sometimes it has to be dug out, word by word, sometimes it is all-engulfing, dramatic, heart-rending, of vital importance.

The *Evening Gazette* is a local newspaper, covering in depth the local scene, but if the story is big enough — from Westminster or the West Indies, the Gazette must publish it, within the hour. But the *Gazette* is also an important Teesside public forum and a shop window for the whole area. It is at once fast and complex and time-dependent. The staff will tell you its daily production is miraculous. But it is also helped by some of the best staff and most modern technical and computer equipment in Britain. This is a little peep behind-the-scenes at Gazette Buildings, Borough Road . . .

On the editorial floor. . . and Tony Dumphy, production editor, and Alan Sims, features editor, discuss a breaking story with some of the reporters and sub-editors hard at work on their screens in the background.

Sub-editor Steve Race puts the finishing touches to a features page on screen. He is able to call in stories and pictures, write, delete, design and create the entire page from his desk. This is modern newspaper production technology at work, with the sub-editor in full control of everything.

Paste-up . . . and stories, headlines, photographs and advertisements are fitted together like a jig-saw. The stories are stuck down on an Evening Gazette grid as it will appear in the paper. When the page is complete it is photographed into negative form. The picture shows the leader page being prepared. The gap on the left is for the editor's editorial. It is still being written.

Last copy, last check by sub-editors for the edition. Okay, let page one go.

Quick now! Last touches in the advertising make-up department where many of the intricate display advertisements are designed, checked and prepared for publication.

It is called the Quiet Room, where the high technology colour press is controlled by the push of a button. It is here that quality control is set and monitored. It may be quiet, but beyond the window the presses are producing their papers with a roar.

Ears muffled against the noise, the colour press gathers speed and another edition of the Evening Gazette is on its way.

Paper up! The Gazette in full flow.

Hot from the Press . . . the papers are stacked ready for delivery.

The Turbulent Fifties

WITH the fearful Forties over, once again the *Gazette* began to gain in strength and reputation. Mr A. J. Josey was the hand guiding the paper from the editorial chair through the two arduous years after the war, before A. L. James took command in 1948. "Chiefy" James remained the *Gazette's* editor for 22 years until his retirement into directorship in 1966. Those transition years when the threads of peace were again being picked up, through the uncertain Fifties and the sad but eventful Sixties, were difficult and perplexing.

One of the most awkward, in a volatile industrial area, was the Kemsley political stance, which the *Gazette* faithfully reflected in its opinion columns. It was so one-sidedly anti-Labour that James was concerned that it could compromise the very veracity of his local news pages. It was an uphill task, but in order to keep his finger on every detail to ensure the fairness of his paper's coverage and be prepared to answer every attack, he even sub-edited all the local election pages himself. In the end he was given the honour of being invited to the Labour Party's victory celebrations.

A.L. James nursed and willed the *Gazette* through many other problems, but perhaps his greatest legacy was the development of the paper's local news platform, area by area, carefully editionised until he had created a local news service unparalleled in Britain. If it's not in the *Gazette* it hasn't happened was a local joke, but it is true little passed the attention of the *Gazette's* news desk and its reporters. James also generally built up an outstanding editorial team of professionals in depth who were highly motivated to make their paper the best evening in the country.

And so the paper came out edition after edition, recording the life of Teesside, the big events that shaped the world, and the community — and the *Gazette's* story.

On June 7, 1956, Viscount Kemsley came to Middlesbrough to set the *Gazette's* new Hoe and Crabtree press roaring out 40,000 copies an hour from this giant capable of producing 32-page papers.

In January, 1958, the Duke of Kent, who was stationed at Catterick as the assistant-adjutant of the Royal Scots Greys, arrived to admire the modern *Gazette* going to press, and in June of the same year a regional readership survey conducted by the Newspaper Society indicated that the *Gazette* was the ladies' favourite with 69 per cent of all the housewives in the North Riding reading it, and 78 per cent in Middlesbrough itself.

It was February 1959, before the *Gazette* was able to change from its wartime tabloid austerity size to the old pre-war broadsheet. The reasons for the return to the old format, listed in a page one story, reflected the growth of the area — and the *Gazette.* "We are back to our pre-war size", said the *Gazette,* "because the tabloid

A Day to Remember

After the splendour and moving moments of the Coronation, the mind, like a kaleidoscope, retains a host of pictures.

To the thousands who braved the long night through the rigours of winter in June, the abiding memory might be one of a sudden, lifting excitement, rising to crescendo as the magnificence of Elizabeth the Second, smiling and bejewelled, rode by in her golden coach. Truly, we can be proud of this mid-century day. If this nation and those of a thrilled and equally-loyal Commonwealth seize opportunity with courage, great things will be accomplished.

June 2, 1953

Sadness . . . as the Evening Gazette reports the death of the King.

restrictions made it impossible to expand any further — and expand we must to keep pace with the demands of the post-war development of industry and business in North Yorkshire and South Durham. Because the calls on our space grow month by month, as we attempt to mirror the fuller life and widespread activities of this fast-growing district. Because the attempt to crowd all the day's news into the small pages often entailed the use of smaller type than readers found convenient. Now the paper will be easier and clearer to read."

From the readers, now grown accustomed to the old size, there was protest. Memories were short, the *Gazette*

Joy . . . as the new Queen visits Teesside for the first time

was like an old friend, and they did not want it changed. At first the management was deeply concerned, but then it was found that the greatest argument against the new look was that the *Gazette* had become more difficult to read in bed, and all the other benefits so outweighed this problem, that the objection was smiled into insignificance.

In the light of what was to follow it was indeed a small complaint. Soon the readers were to have no newspaper at all.

The Thomson Formula

I T WAS, June, 1959 when a series of events began that shook the *Evening Gazette*. The first came on June 6. The recurring rumblings and threats of a national stoppage by the print unions at last became depressing fact and the news came that the paper's proud record of never having missed a day's publication, in spite of three wars and the General Strike, was over. "This is a sad day for the *Evening Gazette*", said a page one announcement. "Due to circumstances of which our readers are well aware, we are compelled to suspend publication for an indefinite period."

That "indefinite period" was, in fact, six-and-a-half weeks. News, of course, stops for no man, but there was no *Gazette* to record it. The *Gazette* office was silent, the bustle gone. The readers, a life-long habit disrupted, were patient, but without their *Gazette* life was, inexplicably, somehow empty. The *Gazette* did its best to keep them informed by issuing typed bulletins containing general and sporting news at regular intervals throughout the day outside head and branch offices, but nothing was quite the same.

The second major shock came barely two weeks after the printers' strike had been resolved. A disconcerting rumour began to whisper its devious way through the newspaper world. Journalists, with a nose ultra-developed to detect a story, became suspicious that the future of the great bastion house of Kemsley was in doubt.

Nothing definite. Nothing to indicate that all was not well. But there was something. The doubt became a whisper, grew to a talking point until it was being discussed freely throughout the length of Britain that possibly, just possibly, the Kemsley empire might have a change of ownership.

But why, and when and to whom?

The Mirror group, it was said, was known to have an interest. The Beaverbrook press had nurtured thoughts of expansion. Or could it be an outsider? Or was it all no more than speculation? The same rumour had also sneaked its way to Middlesbrough, the same questions asked, the same blank faces met the questions. There was the same unease.

The news broke on August 21. It was shattering. Viscount Kemsley had resigned. Kemsley Newspapers, along with the *Evening Gazette*, had a new owner. Roy Thomson.

What it meant was that the *Evening Gazette* had come under the control of a most extraordinary newspaper proprietor.

Blunt, affable, incisive, fast-talking, Roy Herbert Thomson ("call me Roy"), was collecting newspapers at the time of the Kemsley takeover with all the fastidious dedication of a stamp collector.

A Canadian of Scots ancestry, he burst into the staid British newspaper scene with the biting freshness of a gusting prairie breeze, offering to buy any newspaper whose owner was willing to sell.

The astonished Press and the public in

Take-over by Lord Thomson . . .

general, accustomed to the traditional boardroom image of serene dignity and gentility, did not quite know how to take this brash, back-slapping, outspoken, pushing, middle-aged Canuck, with his pebble glasses, crumpled suits, broad grin and flourishing cheque book. But there was no misunderstanding what he said: and he said plenty, to anyone who had a newspaper to sell and would listen, and even to those who had no newspaper to sell and would not listen. His message was direct and to the point: I will buy.

Born in a terraced cul-de-sac house in mid-town Toronto in 1894, his father a barber and his mother a one-time hotel maid, Lord Thomson began his newspaper career by selling them as a boy on Sundays. At 13, he worked his way through a business college by staying back at night to sweep out the classrooms, fill the ink wells, dust the desks, and clean the blackboards. His family was poor, he was myopic, shy, almost introverted, a most unlikely millionaire-to-be. But he also had an extraordinary flair for figures, a cool head for a business deal, a genius and relish for trading, and a thriftiness that later became legendary. His early ventures gave little indication that the future was to be auspicious. Failed farmer, for him a purgatory quickly ended; bankrupt car spares salesman; pedlar of radios in Ontario's far north; eventually a radio station of his own, built on promissory notes, overdrafts, final demands, bland audacity and, without question, the firm indications of financial genius.

His thinking was logical. Better reception from local radio would sell more radio sets, and that would bring in more advertising to pay for it. The plan was sound, the results unrewarding. It meant go broke or expand, so he opened a second station in gold-mining Timmins, and because there happened to be a newspaper in the same building, he bought it too. Perhaps it was not quite as simple as that, for newspapers had always fascinated him, and doubtless, sooner or later, he would have acquired one. But it was the start, and for those with a taste for chronology and the importance of small events, the very first one was the Timmins Press, $6,000 dollars worth of weekly stodge that Thomson vowed to improve.

A year later he turned it into a daily and

it began to flourish, backboned by healthy advertising. He bought more, then even more, and never looked back. By 1950 he was president of the Canadian Daily Newspaper Association, with 23 newspapers under his belt, and a reputation for revamping the traditionally slow-to-change publishing business, introducing many new technical ideas and methods, and sending little cold shiver warning signals down the backs of suddenly apprehensive newspaper proprietors. It was obvious Thomson was a go-getter who would be difficult to stop.

Of course he did not become a millionaire by the time he was 30 as he had once predicted with characteristic precocity, but it was only a deal or two distant, and the experiences that uncovered the skills that moulded the success, as well as the agonies and ecstasies of the chase, made him one of the most formidable business men in the world. Although the manner in which he survived those early days will always be regarded as miraculous, slowly he began to repay his debts, to consolidate, to profit, then to expand and at last to lift his horizon beyond the confines of Canada to Britain.

In 1953 *The Scotsman* in Edinburgh gave him his first toehold in this country, perhaps the most difficult transaction of his life, for *The Scotsman* is a hallowed Scottish institution in the very heart of the Capital of Scotland, a newspaper with a kind of national ownership acknowledged, and the Scots do not give up their prizes easily. If he can win *The Scotsman,* said the publishing world, he can win anything, and a great unease began to spread through British newspaper houses.

Not for a moment did Thomson relent with his talk of money-making, his consuming passion in the economics of newspapers, advertising, costings, budgets, minimising losses, maximising profits. He even boasted balance sheets were his bed-time reading. All his discussions and comments were made with eyebrow-raising frankness that sent takeover warning bells jangling.

But first he turned his attention to commercial television. It was then in its uncertain infancy, and in 1957, with considerable courage, few friends, and amid prophecies of woe and gloom, he launched Scottish Television out of Glasgow's old Theatre Royal, and promptly made himself

> "Roy, I am going to say something to you I have never thought I'd say to anyone", said Lord Kemsley. "I'm going to offer you the Kemsley newspapers. . ."

Lord Kemsley

a million. With STV running smoothly and surplus fast mounting, Thomson was again able to concentrate on his newspapers and his dreams. Only now he was in a hurry. Because the George Outram group, which owned the *Glasgow Herald, Evening Times* and a number of weeklies, fiercely resisted his overtures to sell out, he peremptorily decided to try to take them over by a direct bid to the shareholders. On the morning of July 1, 1959, with the offers printed, sealed, addressed and stamped, waiting only delivery to the post office, Thomson sat at his desk checking the document for the last time, when the telephone rang. Casually he picked it up. Interest flickered. In the history of newspapers few telephone calls can have had such dramatic and far-reaching effects. The timing was perfect, the portent enormous. That telephone call changed Lord Thomson's life, and it brought the *Evening Gazette*, Middlesbrough, into his camp. Lord Kemsley was speaking.

That evening Lord Thomson with his managing director and friend, James Coltart, caught the London sleeper. They checked into the Savoy, and after a 3s 6d breakfast in a favourite lorry drivers' cafe in Covent Garden (the chairman always practised personal parsimony as an example to all) Thomson went to Lord Kemsley's stately office sharp for 10.25am, still wondering which paper in the Kemsley empire he was to be offered. He did not have long to wait for an answer.

"Roy, I'm going to say something to you I never thought I'd say to anyone," said Lord Kemsley. "I'm going to offer you Kemsley newspapers. I've got 40 per cent of the ordinary shares, and I want £6 a share for myself and for any of my minority shareholders who might also want to sell."

Even as he received this stunning information, Thomson's mind was calculating. Figures remembered from a previous Kemsley sound-out. Adding,

guessing, estimating, chancing, heart racing, mind fluttering. All those papers — and *The Sunday Times* too. And the building. And then the chill as his lightning arithmetic told him that it was just too much, that he could not raise the money, even by selling everything he owned. So he said so, his answer calculated almost as soon as the proposition had been completed, and Lord Kemsley suggested that he should talk to his financial advisers, and he would see his, and perhaps something could be worked out.

Thomson left Kemsley House, face inscrutable behind the thick-lensed glasses, but tense with excitement. At Television House he picked up James Coltart, and with a casual "Let's go get some lunch", spirited him away out of earshot. Even in the lift they had company and could not speak, but Coltart detected by Thomson's simmering restraint that something momentous was afoot. They made their way to a restaurant across the road. It was at the pedestrian crossing, amid the roar of traffic and bumping bustle of hurrying people, that Thomson made his revelation.

"It's everything, Jim. Everything. *The Sunday Times* as well."

Where's that put the Outram deal?", asked Coltart, who knew that the offers were to be sent the following morning. "Off!", said Thomson tersely.

The New Look

WHAT followed is newspaper history. Kemsley's passed into Thomson's hands after nine days of the most intricate financial gyrations, climaxed by an amazing reverse bid that finally clinched the deal, in which Kemsley bought STV, paying Thomson with Kemsley shares of such voting power that Thomson controlled the combined Kemsley and STV forces. It was a breathtaking piece of financial expertise, surpassed only by the breathtaking assurance of Lord Thomson when he telephoned Ian MacDonald of the National Commercial Bank of Scotland, with the whole transaction in the balance, and politely asked if he could borrow three million pounds.

At one stroke, Lord Thomson had become what he had always wanted to be — a national newspaper proprietor. When the details were finalised and the announcements made, the magnitude of his position and the responsibilities that went with it were deeply felt. As the *Evening Gazette* staff heard the news of the takeover and speculation about the future flared, Lord Thomson sent the paper this special message:

"This moment, when I assume control of such an important and progressive group of newspapers, is one of great pride for me. It is also a source of much satisfaction to me that this transfer of control has been carried through in such a friendly manner.

"At the same time, I approach my new responsibilities with great humility, even though I have had many years of experience in the journalistic world.

"The newspapers of the group published outside London serve some of the most important and flourishing regions in Britain. Each of these papers has for many years played an important role in the communal life of the area — recording, interpreting and influencing.

"I shall ensure, so far as I can, that the *Evening Gazette* will not only continue to play that role in North Yorkshire and South Durham, but will be encouraged and supported in expanding and developing it so that it may keep pace with — and indeed lead — the expansion and developing of its own communities.

"That intention arises from my firm conviction that a regional Press in vigorous health is essential to the public well-being of Britain. The primary responsibility rests upon editors, and it has always been my policy to give them the greatest possible freedom of action to further the interests for their communities and their papers. That policy I propose to continue in the group, in which, I should add, it will be no new development.

"There are great days ahead for newspapers, for there is still no medium with wider authority than the printed word. Those who create newspapers share a great privilege, for they are heirs to a tradition which must be jealously maintained."

The Thomson impact was immediate. Not at first discernible to the readers because editorially the *Gazette* did not appear different, except that there was wider editorial freedom and the paper's political policy became independent rather than toeing the Tory line.

The major change was in commercial thinking, and the introduction of new

The power of advertising at the Grand Opera House, Middlesbrough, at the turn of the century.

management structures, skills and objectives.

It was part of the Thomson philosophy that only a newspaper in robust financial health was a viable proposition in the long term. Already he had anticipated that epidemic of newspaper sickness that wrought so many casualties in the Sixties, and cast doubt about the continued life of others in the Seventies. He knew with sadness, as only an editor and proprietor can know, that every time a newspaper dies, a little freedom and democracy die with it. Even in this country, he believed, freedom remained a delicate bloom and it was Thomson's firm conviction that freedom's best interests were served by producing vigorous, inquisitive, independent newspapers that were also financial successes to provide necessary stability.

Bearing this in mind, he set about

establishing that stability and one of the obvious ways of achieving it was through advertising. After all, long before Lord Thomson came to Britain, he had perfected the techniques of newspaper advertising services to a science. If anyone knew its worth, how to attract it and provide the right platform for the best result, it was Lord Thomson.

His first priority was to reorientate the *Gazette's* advertising ideas into unison with his own and to give his staff more confidence, more importance and status. Over the already successful *Gazette* sales systems he superimposed his own formulae, adding a touch of Canadian belligerence, but so disciplined and restrained and acceptable to the more sophisticated British advertiser that it soon became clear a new and potent commercial force had arrived in this country.

Pills, Potions, Profit

THE story of advertising, of course, from the first inhibited one-by-one shyly advocating in Saxon Black type the use of home-made secret powders and potions to soothe boils or horse colic in the year 1600, to today's flamboyant, poet-inspired, dream-visualised full-page art forms, is a fascination.

As well as reflecting the changing face of society, the styles, crazes, fears, inventions, social patterns and psychology of people, the study of the advertisments through the years is a ready guide to the state of the nation.

When the *Gazette* was first published, a man's overcoat cost 16s 6d, and a suit of best quality could be bought for 13s. Ladies' long cloth tucked drawers trimmed with needlework sold for 1s 8d, and if she did not like the needlework, they cost her 5d less. A private fitting room was at the customer's disposal to try on guinea-gold lucky 22ct wedding rings for 10s 6d. Champagne cost 3s 6d a bottle, delicious fresh-churned margarine was 4d a pound, finest butter 10d.

In 1882 a Middlesbrough store offered to furnish a working man's house throughout, starting in the kitchen: table, four chairs, couch, fender, and fire irons, four engravings, clock, pots, pans, kettles, crockery; first bedroom: iron bedstead and mattress, flock bed, dressing table, and wash-stand, chest of drawers, two chairs, toilet glass, toilet set, fender, towel rail, two pictures, blinds, rollers and curtains; second bedroom — iron bedstead and mattress, flock bed, dressing table, one chair, toilet glass, blind. The total cost for the whole house was £10.

Even doctors were forced to advertise for patients in the early days in an attempt to remain in business against the growing tide of magical pills, ointment, lotions, embrocations, cordials, elixers, regularity correctives and the whole panacea of quackery that sought out the *Gazette* to inform potential customers.

At the turn of the century, Mr S. E. Smith, the aural surgeon from Newcastle, booked a thrice weekly four-by three in the *Gazette* extolling his virtues. Surgeon Smith's casebook listed sundry patients, nameless, but suitably near death, who had either been cured or were successfully under treatment for such horrifics as "deafness, speechlessness, fearful discharges, noises in the head and ears, morbid growths and other interesting cases". He consulted between 11 am and 3 pm daily.

The classified want ads were quick to impinge on the market. One of the first to appear in the *Gazette* sought applications from an "active female servant". It cautioned that "none need apply without their character, and cleanliness must bear the strictest investigation". It cost the advertiser 2d.

The jingoists were at work even in 1869, and for a penny a man could buy instant wellbeing with a pint of "Herb Beer, the temperance drink that has no peer". And if he lost his hat in the revelry, he could always visit Henderson the Hatter of Linthorpe Road, Middlesbrough, who took a double column to announce that he was "a valuable addition to the head trade in England".

The *Evening Gazette's* advertisement

department in those early days was hardly geared for the big sell. Until the time of the Berry takeover much confidence was placed in the postman, and the department in the mid-Thirties consisted of one advertisement manager, two counter girls for the smalls, and three representatives, each equipped with his own bicycle. In 1935, the rate per single column inch was 5s.

Under the Berry brothers, of course, advertising had been developed, but it was left to Lord Thomson to introduce undreamed of dimensions. Part of his business credo had always been that the advertiser must get the best possible service. It included personal attention and expert advice when required to give the advertiser maximum result for his money. Lord Thomson lost no time in moving towards this aim on the *Gazette.* Quickly he injected new ideas and refinements of his own, soared morale and more than doubled the staff, who suddenly became impassioned and crusading in the belief of the power and quality of their service.

Although a two-girl Tele-ad service for the convenience of the small advertisers

had been started in 1958 under Lord Kemsley, in 1961 Thomson made a major reorganisation in the front office to accommodate what amounted to an entirely new department, now consisting of 30 highly-trained specialists, who provided one of the finest advertising services in the country.

The six-man display department was also massively developed in size and importance, and soon the column inches came rolling in, more and more, faster and faster.

But still Thomson was not satisfied, still he felt that there was scope for improved services and the building of greater trust and respect between advertiser and the *Evening Gazette* and its staff. So he launched the entirely new concept at the time of a promotions department, where a staff of marketing experts, visualisers, writers and artists were on hand to discuss, advise and assist clients in discovering the best use and form of their advertising and sales promotion.

And, of course, like so many other Thomson innovations, it proved an outstanding success.

All Change

IT WAS veteran managing director George Pratt who initiated the first firm steps in what was to be a dynamic new era of newspaper change. The Thomson success formula was based on a positive and professional management style, with emphasis on managing the business aspects of the *Evening Gazette,* as well as producing the best evening paper possible. George had seen out the old days, altering wisely the shape and pace of the paper to meet changing circumstances and demands. Now the *Gazette* was entering a new era of vigorous change in everything on the newspaper in dramatically changing times. When George Pratt's time came to retire in 1964, after 26 years in the managerial chair, he left the *Evening Gazette* rather as he found it — in a hectic welter of new building programmes with the rattle of pneumatic drills echoing along Borough Road as a tasteful major extension was added to the office. Twice during his career on the *Gazette* he had witnessed his newspaper outgrow its premises, reflecting the growth of Teesside itself. It was also expanding in Stockton, and on the day of his retiral George Pratt saw his plans for the total reconstruction of the Brunswick Street branch office reach fruition to give the *Gazette* further strategic importance in that area.

During those 26 years George Pratt had seen the industrial might of the area develop with steel and petro chemical-based industries and their spin-offs and the River Tees growing increasingly important as a port. New housing developments were springing up on the periphery of Teesside's towns and out into the villages beyond — in Billingham, Stockton, Yarm, Marton, Guisborough, Great Ayton, Redcar, Saltburn and even out at Stokesley and Hutton Rudby. Change was being written right across the face of the whole area. And along with Teessiders spreading out from their old close-knit communities, into those new homes came outsiders, ICI and British Steel managers at every level and their workforces. Not since the mad days of the iron rush had there been a process of such sustained change. It was not just physical, but also change in outlook and priorities — and there was also a renewed sense of challenge.

It was the birth of Teesside as a county borough in 1966 that gave focus to the changes. The old town and county rivalries

Mr George Pratt Managing Director 1938 - 1964

Mr Leslie James, Editor 1948 - 1966

Mr Leonard Harton Managing Director 1964 - 1969

Full story of Cannon-street disturbances unfold

GAOL SENTENCES PASSED ON 16 MEN

Stern Bench warning

SENTENCING 16 people to prison in Middlesbrough this afternoon for their part in weekend "violence and hooliganism", the Stipendiary Magistrate, Mr A. P. Peaker, said: "I hope that, these sentences having been passed and order restored, there will be no more trouble on any future occasion".

He intended, he said, to deal with any such offences in future with the utmost rigour. The police were determined to stop such behaviour and the Bench intended to support them.

Mr Peaker, who also ordered five young men to spend varying times in detention centres, said: "Of all the time I have been in Middlesbrough I have not had such a disgraceful state of affairs as I have to deal with today. It makes the position in the town intolerable".

Middlesbrough's Chief Constable, Mr Ralph Davidson, said at one-o'clock this morning at a Press conference: "In my view this is not truly a racial dispute. It is very obvious from the type of person taking part, that it is not primarily a dispute that is racial in character".

How the Gazette reported the Cannon Street riots and their aftermath on August 21, 1961.

In the early 1960s Tees shipbuilding was still a force. The picture shows the keel and shell of a 26,400-ton sulphur carrier under construction at the Furness Shipyard, Haverton Hill.

General Sir Brian Horrocks, accompanied by managing director Leonard Harton, starts up the press on a visit to the new Gazette office in 1965.

The linotype machine was still king when Lord Kenneth Thomson visited the Gazette's caseroom in 1963 where the newspaper type was set in hot metal on the big machines.

of North Yorkshire and South Durham suddenly appeared less significant, the new infant Teesside seemed bigger, stronger and of greater joint potential than its individual towns with their old local loyalties could achieve alone. Suddenly Teesside was full of excitement again — and aspiration.

The Evening Gazette, sensing the change of mood and recognising the new opportunity, hailed Teesside and gave it full support.

It even commissioned Poet Laureate Cecil Day Lewis to versify on the subject for the great occasion.

Middlesbrough and its close neighbours along the Tees had developed around its industries and were wedded to its various works. They had no pretence at being anything other than industrial towns and they were proud of it. But now there was talk of improving infrastructure and communications, seeking better hotel accommodation, restaurants and quality shopping. All those newcomers began to demand the kind of facilities and services they were accustomed to in London or Manchester or Edinburgh. Of course, things didn't happen overnight, and there were misgivings and sometimes protests, yet in spite of recession, boundary changes and unforeseen pitfalls, there has been an ongoing process ever since and Teesside has, as a place to live, outstripped in its development many other cities in Britain with higher profiles and reputations for sophisticated living, but less quality of life.

The "Old Brigade" of George Pratt and editor Leslie James at last retired and into the *Evening Gazette* at this crucial time, amid the shake, rattle and roar of the builders as the *Gazette's* classy new extension began to take shape, came Mr Leonard Harton as managing director in November 1964 and, two years later, Scotsman Mr William Heeps as editor. It was a team that slammed the changes into top gear and began a period of intense activity in every department of the newspaper. New ideas and fresh approaches went gusting through the office, new faces were recruited from around the country to find still more ideas from outside the Thomson family of newspapers. It was robust and exciting and the *Gazette's* commercial records that once seemed set for ever, began to tumble — in advertising volumes, in through-put of pages and in

1963. . .and this was how Borough Road looked before the Gazette's new extension was built as the paper expanded.

1964. . .the old houses are down, the foundations of the new building are well laid and the hoarding is handy for news bills.

Castro supporter before Grand Jury next week

MAN IS CHARGED WITH MURDERING KENNEDY

Attorney says: He has made no confession

November 23, 1963. . .how the Gazette broke the shock news.

Four of Teesside's most famous citizens of their day joined Mr Kenneth Thomson, as he was then, now Lord Thomson, but at that time president of Thomson Newspapers, Ltd., to a special dinner party in Billingham. They are (from left to right): Sir Charles Fitton, Mr George Pratt, director and manager of the Evening Gazette, Lord Thomson, Sir William Crosthwaite and Alderman C.W Allison.

Gazette editorial staff in the 1960s who

higher circulation figures. In fact, it was during this period that the *Gazette* reached its highest circulation with a daily family of readers in excess of 350,000. Leonard Harton was one of the new breed of professional managers who set out clearly his policy of management by objectives and then set out to achieve them with determination. He had been in charge of the Stockport group of Thomson Newspapers since 1960, and was a former editor of the old *Empire News, South Wales Echo* in Cardiff and the *Sunday Sun* in Newcastle. He was experienced, demanding, forthright and he threw himself into developing the paper and playing his part in the community with characteristic vigour.

William "Bill" Heeps, one of the *Gazette's* most famous "old boys", had a glittering newspaper career that spanned the bottom to the pinnacle of the newspaper business, mastering almost every job in a newspaper office along the way and was eventually awarded a CBE for his services to the industry. His career began as a cub reporter on Falkirk's weekly *Mail*, in his native Scotland, progressing to the top-selling *Daily Record* in Glasgow. But his love of sport took him into sporting journalism on the now defunct *Evening Dispatch* as a sports writer, then sports editor, assistant editor of the Edinburgh *Evening News and Dispatch* and, for a time, he was even a television sports reporter. He was the *Evening Gazette's* editor from 1966-1968, returned in 1972 for three years as managing director, later became editorial director of Thomson Regional Newspapers and finally chairman of the group, one of the biggest and most

Mr William Heeps, CBE, Editor 1966-1968. Managing Director 1972-1975

Mr Richard Parrack, Editor 1968 - 1969

Mr Ian Fawcett, D.S.O., D.F.C., Editor 1969 - 1970

innovative newspaper houses in the country and a director of the International Thomson Organisation.

As editor Bill Heeps also set about further developing the *Evening Gazette* with gusto. His was a campaigning style and he placed the paper fully behind the infant Teesside and played an influential role in its establishment. As part of the hurricane of change to go sweeping through the whole *Gazette* office, Bill Heeps decided on a new and more modern look for the newspaper to keep pace with the optimistic new image of the area. It was immediately judged to be the best-designed evening newspaper in Britain in the Annual Newspaper Design Awards.

Journalistically and in the community the *Gazette* was sparking, the mood volatile. The paper had always enjoyed a reputation

for the quality and spread of its reporting, now it was also being recognised as the paper that got things done in the community. There was never any question about where the *Gazette* stood on any issue — but it was always four-square behind Teesside and the readers recognised it as a stout champion of their causes and the area and one of its most influential voices.

It was also a time of unprecedented executive change on the paper. The days when senior executives like George Pratt and Leslie James remained in their posts for 20 years or more seemed gone forever. Between 1964 and 1970 the *Gazette* had three managing directors and four editors. Bill Heeps was the first to move, off to Wales as managing director of Celtic Press. He was succeeded by the giant Mr Richard Parrack, who was editor of the Lancashire

The Gazette office on Borough Road, Middlesbrough, shortly after the extension was completed. The obvious changes from today are that cars were free to park as long as they liked, the Gazette sign has had a face-lift and the clock is now digital.

This week of mourning

Details given for the lying-in-state

Sir Winston Churchill

THE BRITISH people stood today, proudly but sorrow-fully, at the head of a vast concourse of the nations mourning Sir Winston Churchill.

Since the news of his death, a mighty torrent of tributes has flowed.

The lying in state of Sir Winston in Westminster Hall will be on Wednesday. Today Westminster Hall — usually, dark, dank and echoing — was already filling with an identifiable air of majesty and solemnity.

How the Gazette recorded the passing of a great war-time leader and world statesman on January 25, 1965. And (below) what the Gazette published in its leading article. . .

The incomparable Winston Churchill

SO MANY facets of life, and so many affairs of the world, were graced and invigorated by Sir Winston, that his passing will be felt far beyond the ordinary limits of one man's influence and reputation.

Churchill, the outstanding world statesman of this century, not only made the history of the war years from 1940 to 1945, but himself recorded it in a matchless variety of mood and matter that put history books in the best-seller class, and for those and other monumental tasks in which he was engaged, he deservedly won the Nobel prize for literature.

Painter, racehorse owner, soldier, even bricklayer, Churchill was a man of so many parts. A lesser figure would have been content with success in any one. Churchill was master of them all, an outstanding figure who wouldn't have to wait for history to proclaim his vast contribution to humanity but in his lifetime was judged and acclaimed incomparable.

Beatlecstasy!

One word described the Beatles visit to the Globe Theatre, Stockton. Six girls were treated in hospital for hysteria.

Evening Telegraph, Blackburn, and had a reputation for his professionalism in Newcastle and on the *Daily Express*. Yet it seemed he had no sooner his feet under the table that he was appointed editor of the new computer-set *Evening Post* in Hemel Hempstead, which had been seen as a production step in advance of its time.

Australian Ian Fawcett took over from *The Journal,* in Newcastle, with a distinguished career behind him as a foreign and war correspondent and wide journalistic experience on several newspapers, yet it was some time before the staff discovered he was also a war-time hero, who had been awarded the D.S.O., D.F.C. and Bar and was a squadron leader at the age of 19 in the Royal Australian Air Force.

Every editor, of course, has a different approach, a different method, a different style. Each of these editors brought something with him to the *Gazette* and left something of himself as a professional stamp on the paper.

It was then Mr Harton's turn to move on, a return for him to Newcastle in August 1969, but this time as managing director of the Evening Chronicle and Journal Ltd., the largest centre in Thomson Regional Newspapers.

For those with a taste for coincidences, Mr Harton's successor, three months before the *Gazette* celebrated its 100th birthday in November 1969, was another Scotsman like Sir Hugh Gilzean Reid, the paper's founder a century before him. James S. Adam was also something of an adventurer, with a strong editorial tradition behind him earned on the *Daily Record* in Glasgow and as editor of the *Weekly Scotsman*, in Edinburgh, where Gilzean Reid edited. He was a pioneer of sea canoeing up Scotland's dangerous western seaboard and a lover of mountains. His career had also seen him general manager of The Scotsman Publications Ltd and managing director of The Chester Chronicle and Associated Newspapers Ltd.

And so it was James Adam who took the *Evening Gazette* into its first century, with a new team to steer it into its second, a Scotsman at the helm as the paper began, in high spirits, a track record of success — and eying the future with relish.

A Lusty Centenarian

WHEN the *Evening Gazette* held its centenary celebrations on November 8, 1969, it did so in style. Specially-bottled *Evening Gazette* champagne popped and, in respect of its Scottish founder, Sir Hugh Gilzean Reid, a lone piper played Highland airs from the top of the Gazette's roof to startled Teessiders below. But it was the evening of November 7 that turned into a memorable and glittering occasion to savour. A special centenary banquet was held in the Billingham Arms Hotel and all the dignitaries of Teesside were present to do honour to the lusty centenarian.

Lord Thomson of Fleet, and his son Kenneth, flew in from Toronto, lords and ladies, bishops and knights, mayors, M.P.s, councillors, the familiar faces of local celebrities and some *Gazette* old boys like Sir Denis Hamilton came to pay tribute.

"The *Evening Gazette*", said Lord Thomson, "is known as the Bible of Teesside. It seems to me to be aptly named as it seems to epitomise and represent the very best interests and highest ideals of this rapidly developing and exciting area."

Lord Thomson went on to confirm that the code of Gilzean Reid, made a century earlier, which stated that the *Gazette* would speak out for its readers' rights and defend

them, would continue to be the paper's maxim in the future.

" At the time I acquired the *Gazette*", said Lord Thomson, " I said I hoped it would keep pace with and, indeed, lead the expansion and development of its own community, and I believe it has fulfilled these expectations".

Other speakers also told of the *Gazette's* role in fashioning Teesside. Sir Ray Pennock, chairman of ICI 's Agricultural Division at the time, believed that the paper had been something of a social conscience for the North-east. He suggested that the *Gazette's* duty in the next hundred years was to make Teesside accept it own shortcomings, which was the job of a free Press and a job everyone should welcome in a free society.

The Marquis of Normanby, Lord Lieutenant of the North Riding, declared he was a staunch reader of the *Gazette* and it was not always recognised how big a part the journalist played in the public's thinking. "The reporter", he went on, "could shape, through his newspaper, the views of a large section of the general public and it was obviously a job in which great integrity was required. As far as one can foresee, the future for Teesside is one of growth and prosperity. The *Evening*

Spectacular fireworks displays were part of the countdown to the Evening Gazette's 100th birthday celebrations.

Mr James S. Adam, Managing Director, 1969 - 1972

Gazette can, and will, play a major part in this development.

"I suggest that a function of your development is to try to foster in us independence. It is the basis of our freedom".

There was even a congratulatory telegram from that old warhorse Harold MacMillan, former MP for Stockton and Conservative Prime Minister; and the Bishop of Durham commented on the *Gazette's* renowned liveliness and vigour. It was indeed an occasion to remember, where the community and its newspaper, which had worked so hard together in the interest of the new Teesside, had met,

as Lord Thomson pointed out, in unity of purpose.

That sense of teamsmanship was the clear message of the evening, as if the newspaper and the community, who were also the readers of the *Evening Gazette*, shared a common destiny together.

A few evenings before, on Guy Fawkes night, the sky was lit up with a fireworks display commemorating the *Gazette's* centenary with its name picked out in tall, sparkling letters.

Lord Thomson visited the *Gazette* office to congratulate the staff on the paper's 100th anniversary. He was impressed with the activity in the newsroom — for already they were hard at work getting the paper's next century off to a professional and business–like start.

LATEST NEWS from *The Daily Gazette, 1869 . . .*

ACCIDENT AT THE CLAY LANE IRONWORKS: On Monday morning, Mr Jones, a labourer employed at the Clay lane Ironworks, was engaged in clearing some pieces of coal from under the lift of the blastfurnaces, which was up at the time. Whilst so employed, the lift, for some reason or another, descended, and crushed the unfortunate man severely. When got out it was found he had sustained a fracture of the right leg below the knee, and he was conveyed to the North Riding Infirmary where amputation was pronounced to be necessary.

THE EXTENSIVE SMUGGL-ING CASE: At four o' clock on Saturday afternoon, the captain and crew of the s.s. Glenmore were again charged with smuggling 31 3-16th lbs of tobacco. The board of customs having been communicated with, a telegram in reply was received ordering the ship to be seized. In the course of the afternoon, however, George Redshaw, the mate of the vessel, who had absconded, delivered himself into custody and pleaded guilty. All

the other prisoners were consequently discharged, and Redshaw was remanded until Tuesday

A BOY SEVERELY BURNT: A boy named Patrick Fitzgerald, residing with his parents in Newcastlerow, was, on Saturday last, left with his younger brother in charge of the house. At three o' clock a woman who lives in the house below went in and found him enveloped in flames. Before the fire could be extinguished the boy was severely burnt, and he was taken to the infirmary.

LAUNCH AT MIDDLES-BROUGH: A sloop-rigged vessel, named "The Fox", was launched on Saturday afternoon from the yard of Messrs Backhouse and Dixon, Middles-brough. The new vessel will carry 250 tons, and her dimensions are - length, 108 ft; beam, 20 ft; depth 8ft 9 ins. She has been fitted with high pressure engines, 35 nominal horse power, by Messrs David Joy and Co., and has been built for Messrs Williams and Purvis, Middles-brough.

A JEREMY DIDDLER CAUGHT: At the South Stockton Police Court, this (Monday) morning, Alfred Oliver was brought up on remand, charged with obtaining money on false pretences, on 8th November. George Pearson said the defendant went to him and represented that he was empowered by the masters at the ironworks to ascertain what was owing to shop-keepers, so that it could be deducted from the mens' wages by instalments. He gave him a list of debtors amounting to £4, and 4s commission. Elizabeth McAll, also a grocer at South Stockton, said the defendant went to her shop on Tuesday moning, 9th November, and asked if she had a list of debts unpaid since the strike, and where the men worked who owed them. She replied that her two sons worked at Mr Whitwell's and she had intended seeing him about the matter. Prisoner said he was the agent for Mr Whitewell. Mr Whitwell made affirmation that the prisoner had never received any authority as agent for Thornaby Ironworks, nor was he ever employed in any capacity.

Target Work

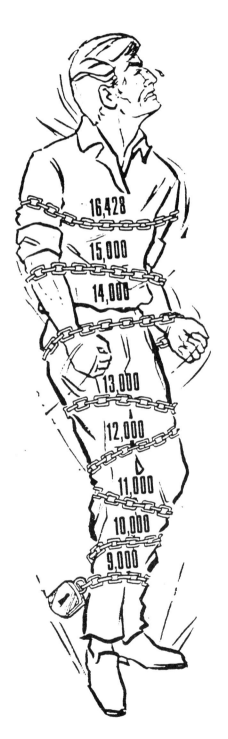

LORD THOMSON'S message at the *Evening Gazette's* centenary dinner, reaffirming the paper's role as a local watchdog and champion of the community, was soon to be vividly demonstrated as the readers were introduced to the chain-bound figure of Joe Jobb.

The first real setback of the new county borough was when early warning signals of recession began to declare themselves and the dole queues lengthened ominously. The economic stop-goes of successive governments was something Teessiders knew only too well to their cost, but rising unemployment was the last thing the aspiring new Teesside needed.

Frustratingly, so much of the problem was outside local influence. Teesside had the workforce, much of it skilled, it had an excellent record of industrial relations — but jobs were vanishing.

As unemployment increased, the *Evening Gazette* decided to try to reverse the trend and go into battle to win or save those jobs.

It was not long before the *Evening Gazette's* powerful headlines and comments on behalf of the area caught the imagination of readers. Enormous support began to rally behind the paper's lead from all quarters and at every level.

By this time editor Ian Fawcett had left Teesside to edit the *Evening Chronicle* in Newcastle and his place as editor of the *Evening Gazette* was taken by his deputy, Mr Ian Nimmo. A period of intense

"Teesside's appalling jobless totals move agonisingly upwards. They are a disgrace in the community. It is intolerable that this area should have to bear such a burden, such a waste of people, such indignity and hardship". It was with these words the Gazette launched one of the most important campaigns in its history in 1972 against the rising tide of unemployment.

JOE JOBB: HOW TO BREAK THE CHAINS

Gazette headline after its successful public debate in the Town Hall

campaigning followed with the emphasis firmly on improving the quality of life in Teesside and speaking out for the whole area.

When Ian Nimmo launched the "Target Work" campaign no one envisaged quite where it might lead. If it won jobs and helped stem the flow of losses, it was felt, that was a positive outcome. But suddenly it was realised the whole community was associating with the *Gazette's* stance, uniting in the call for work. And it soon became clear large headlines, thundering editorials and embarrassing politicians just wasn't enough. Expectations were raised and there had to be a more tangible outcome.

Firstly, the paper called a public meeting, chaired by the editor, which filled Middlesbrough Town Hall to overflowing, with one of the best political debates in many years.

A campaign of major stories, investigative articles, features and editorials were mounted, putting those who could influence jobs in the area firmly on the spot. *The Gazette's* "Target Work" campaign soon introduced readers to a symbol figure of Joe Jobb, a shirt-sleeved Teesside worker in chains, published full length on page one. Every turn of the chain carried a jobless total beside it and a large padlock added to his misery. The aim of the campaign was to get the chains off Joe and set him free to work.

Then Stockton businessman Mr George Sundell, in one of the many letters that flooded into the paper, suggested a train be hired and filled with the unemployed to

Gazette calls forum on jobs ...the platform party in the Town Hall in April 1972 included (from the left): John Harvey-Jones, the chairman of ICI Wilton; Labour M.P. Bill Rodgers; Alderman Ronald Hall, Harold Walker, Shadow Employment Secretary; Conservative MP John Sutcliffe and Harold Robson, Middles-brough district secretary, Amalgamated Union of Engineering Workers. The headline read: "600 vent their fury as the experts search for a solution".

take their demands to Westminster. Good idea! But the *Gazette* also considered the begging-bowl image for an area with so much to offer was the wrong approach.

The Gazette was being caught up in its own success and, as the movement grew in momentum, it was discovered "Target Work" was bigger than the paper alone. The whole community was speaking. So Mr Nimmo formed a "Target Work" committee, which as editor he chaired, and included industrial editor Michael Morrissey and leading Teessiders — and the Jobless Express was on the rails.

Everyone wanted to play a role, from Mayor Ron Hall to Sir John Harvey-Jones, then chairman of ICI Wilton. So the paper set up a series of six target lobbies, each led by a top calibre local executive or businessman. The "targets" were advised well in advance and they all agreed to co-operate fully. The lobbies were briefed individually by their respective chairmen and each had a plan of action, a list of requirements and a detailed description of what Teesside had to offer in return for their work.

The targets had been fine-tuned by the committee: 1. The go-ahead for the Redcar steel complex, with a bonus of a

possible 10,000 jobs; 2. Saving the threatened Eaglescliffe naval depot; 3.Oil terminals, in particular the Phillips Petroleum complex at Seal Sands; 4. More training for jobless youngsters; 5. Government departments to be transferred to Teesside; 6. A university for the area.

The railway platform was crowded. The train pulled in. Four-hundred-and-fifty Teessiders piled on. Industrialists, top businessmen, councillors, trade unionists, managers, workers and unemployed. Off they sped with their causes. Then the dignified march through the streets of London on Westminster, the editor of the *Evening Gazette* and the Mayors of Teesside and Hartlepool out front.

Teesside's M.P.s — and other M.P.s from all parties —ushered the throng into the

Give Teesside a chance, Ted!

Prime Minister Edward Heath was told this afternoon that the Target Work Lobby was not in London with begging bowls, but armed with positive ideas and suggestions.

The news was sent to him by letter when the Jobs Express reached London from Teesside at lunchtime.

The Prime Minister was told: We have many strengths. We have one of the best and biggest labour forces in the country as well as the finest management-union relationships in Britain."

The letter, dictated by Evening Gazette editor and lobby chairman, Mr Ian Nimmo, ended "We are confident there is much we can do for you and the country. We ask you to give us the opportunity".

Above: Look out London, here we come …Target Work's dignified lobby marches on Westminster

Left: How Gazette reporter John McLeod began his story on Teesside's mission to find jobs.

House of Commons where the points at issue were discussed seriously one by one. Some had thought the lobby impossible to organise. Teesside and the *Gazette* showed them how it could be done!

A further group, led by George Sundell, delivered a letter to Prime Minister Ted Heath in 10 Downing Street, which had been composed by the editor on the train and typed by *Gazette* reporter John McLeod. It set out Teesside's case logically, rationally, forcefully — and with conviction. What it asked for was opportunity.

The first three targets on the list were direct hits. It was Sir John Harvey-Jones' lobby, confronting Industrial Development Minister Chris Chataway, that brought the importance of Ekofisk to the Minister's attention and it came to Teesside rather than Emden.

Others were partial successes or took longer to mature than was desirable at the time. Of course, no one was going to admit

that the lobby was responsible for the successes, but it concentrated the minds of those who made the decisions and brought the arguments home to them powerfully. "Target Work" certainly played its part. And slowly, by whispers, leaks and winks, it became clear that it had played a large part.

The new managing director of the *Gazette* was also involved by chairing a lobby. Mr James Adam had retired, and former editor Bill Heeps, who had done so much campaigning himself on the community's behalf, quickly in these circumstances felt thoroughly and entirely at home.

Some national newspapers called "Target Work" a latter day Jarrow March. *The Gazette* never really saw it in that light. There were few similarities other than the need for work. But what it did do — and the paper underlined the point — it demonstrated that Teesside united, newspaper and community together, was indeed a formidable joint force.

*Below:
Ready for the
big day
. . . one of
Teesside's
jobless army in
May, 1972,
young Sean
Kavanagh,
then aged 18,
with some of
the Target
Work posters
prepared for the
march on
Westminster.*

NOW WE ARE ON OUR WAY

THEY SAID it couldn't be done. The advice from the experts was drop the idea, it is impossible, impracticable and you will not get the support.

But on Thursday the Target Work London Lobby heads south by special express and aboard is the finest representative gathering of job hunters that Teesside has ever had.

Never before in our experience has a whole community — industrialists, managements, trade unions, the unemployed, town councillors, businessmen, bankers, teachers, churchmen, solicitors, M.P.s, indeed almost the whole spectrum of Teesside's society — joined together in common purpose, hired a train and set off for London to do something about the area's problem.

It is an astonishing example of community self-help of the highest possible order. It also demonstrates the worth, the sinew and the determination of the area to succeed. It is truly remarkable.

From the Gazette, May, 1972

Memory Lane

AS IF in acknowledgementof the *Evening Gazette's* centenary year the paper published one of the biggest stories of the century on July 21, 1969. The quiet American astronauts Neil Armstrong and Edwin Aldrin had made that giant step for mankind and stood on the surface of the moon.

The *Gazette's* front page headline summed it up in a quote by one of the astronauts — "Boy, isn't this something!". It was a newsman's dream except for the lack of pictures. Like other newsapers the *Gazette* reluctantly took photographs from the live transmissions from the moon on television, but the quality was poor and it was frustrating to record such an event without giving detail of the very thing most people wanted to see — the surface of the moon.

But the *Gazette* linked with its sister paper, the *Evening Post* in Reading, which had colour printing facilities, and a special issue was published with stunning colour photographs to continue the early

pioneering work in this type of publication. *Moon Landing*, with an appropriate space-age type face for the title, contained 20 pages, sold for 6d, the photographs were so sharp you could see the astronauts' footprints clearly in the moon dust — and it sold out.

The unbeatable combination of big stories with full colour was not lost on the *Gazette*, which stored away the idea for future use, but it is interesting to note that experimental colour supplements before their time were appearing in the paper 25 years ago.

Teesside was booming and the *Gazette* with it. The paper entered its second century in sprightly form, yet success often brings its own problems. The size of the paper had been increasing and the brunt of coping with rising volumes of advertising and editorial fell on the production department. It became clear it was stretched to the limit. The presses were incapable of running more than 32 pages and there were

BOY, ISN'T THIS SOMETHING!

As the men on the moon said ...

APOLLO II astronauts Neil Armstrong and Edwin Aldrin clambered safely back into their moonship early today after leaving man's first footprints on the surface of the moon.

Back on Eagle, the astronauts are now asleep. But flight surgeons said heart tests showed that if Armstrong was sleeping at all it was a fitful sleep.

Centenary year first . . . the Gazette's front page story covering man's historic landing on the moon. Far left: the special colour supplement to mark the event that was ahead of its time.

occasions when the maximum size was being produced four days a week, with large papers on every other day. Even in the early 1970s, it was clear a time would come when the *Gazette* would have to substantially re-equip.

Big papers, big stories, high circulation, staff working flat out, but enjoying the journalism. At that time the paper had a happy blend of old timers and young thrusters, with old hands 'memories reaching back to the early part of the century. And like all good newspapers it had its full share of characters sprinkled throughout the building. Harry Lonsdale was "Old Faithful's" driver, the *Gazette's* first Model "T" Ford, ferrying newspapers on the Newport Road, Stockton and Thornaby run back in the 1920s. His was a *Gazette* family and his son Norman became the respected works engineer, although at one time he had been the driver of the editorial department's fancy-looking Morris Cowley.

The *Gazette* drivers have always taken pride in getting the paper through, no matter the weather, in spite of the dales in winter being capable of producing Arctic conditions. Shortly after the war, Mrs Doris McElligot, who was delivering on the Whitby coast road, became well and truly stuck in a snowdrift and spent three days in a cut-off farmhuse before being rescued. Of

course, she had first delivered her last papers. To get the *Gazette* out to its readers a combination of horse-drawn cabs, motorbikes, barrows, bicycles, sledges, taxis, news boys and girls have been adopted over the years. It is said the *Gazette's* horse-drawn vehicles had other dignified duties to perform — like attending at funerals, but discreetly the details are not recorded.

Even in the early days getting the paper out was always done at break-neck speed to catch the trains. The *Gazette's* big newspaper barrows were two-wheelers, a boy between the shafts and another at the back pushing mightily. They would load up and sprint with a rumble for the railway station, where the staff were waiting and the gates open to take them directly to the platform. Sometimes they were still hurling parcels on to the train as it was moving out. Even with four-page papers in those days the Gazette's maxim of "The latest with the best" was taken with deadly seriousness.

The final *Sports Gazette* hit the streets at 7 p.m. on Saturdays. All the football results and reports came to the Post Office by telegraph, and the telegraph boys were waiting at the ready to dash to the *Gazette* office. On those occasions when the Boro was defeated, the shouts of "Run, run, run, there are trains to be caught" chased them down the road. It was frequently a close-

Country living . . .this was Acklam Road at the turn of the century. Getting the Gazette into the country areas along unmade roads was often a horse-and -buggy job.

The height of diversion . . .Redcar's Promenade provided almost everything a family could want in the Old Days, including the Gazette to read on the beach, but times changed and even the dancing in the pier ballroom went out of fashion and in the end the pier itself was demolished.

Ready for battle. . .the Gazette cricket team of 1929 and its support on an outing to face the might of Bishop Auckland.

Another time another place. . . the Gazette stalwarts of 1976 do battle with a rustic 11 from the Pot and Glass at Egglescliffe.

Mountains of paper, not a screen to be seen. . .the sub-editors' table in action in 1984, but where have all the glue pots gone?

run affair, because the first train departed only 15 minutes after the paper was due to print.

Michael "Mick" Keegan was one of the *Gazette's* characters who began his 40 years on the paper in the 1890s. Entertainer, poet, lyricist, publicity manager and circulation manager, perhaps his main claim to fame was his "invention" of the *Sports Gazette's* scoreboard at football matches, which was copied by other newspapers throughout the country. With the help of an old mangle handle and a crank wheel, the contraption was winched into place after the appropriate scores had been hung on nails beside the correct key letter. This brilliant idea received a grateful bonus of a half-crown added to his 30 shillings-a-week pay packet. It was another of those *Gazette* family affairs because Mick's son, Vin Keegan, followed in his father's footsteps to give the paper many years of long and dedicated sevice.

In those far-off days the compositors arrived for work in bowler hats and chewed tobacco or camomile at their linotype machines because smoking was forbidden. At election times, the *Gazette's* Zetland Road office showed the latest results by lantern slides in the window. A crowd always gathered and brawls between rival camps were regarded almost as normal.

The *Gazette* was always fortunate with the calibre of its district reporters, men of worth and standing in the community. Theirs was a dedicated job, on call 24 hours a day, recognised as authorities on their patches and known by every resident. They were able to maintain their status simply because of their professionalism and the accuracy of their stories. They knew everyone and everything that was going on and local people turned to them for advice and assistance. Such men were Bill Newton at Northallerton, Tom Leonard in Guisborough and Tom Ashworth at Whitby. In their local communities they were kings and visiting editors were soon told by readers who really was in charge of the *Gazette*. In the 1960s and 70s they gave the paper sterling coverage.

There were other editorial characters on the *Gazette* at that time who lent it colour. Like Hector Thomson, the features editor, who must have been one of the last journalists in Britain to use an old-fashioned eyeshade; Syd Jackson, the news editor and

authority on matters current and historical in the area; or Walter Greenwood, the assistant news editor, who had such passion for railway time tables he could recite train arrival, departure and connection times around the country; Cliff Mitchell, the sports editor; wee Scotsman John McLeod, the investigative reporter, who boasted a Special Branch tie and also a Holybush tie after a Skelton murder inquiry; Mick Tarte, the talented reporter and leader writer, who tragically died in a drowning accident; Big Roy Madison, the features editor who strolled Madison Avenue daily along the editorial corridor, now long gone; that formidable interviewer and industrial editor Mike Morrissey; Liz Scotston, the women's editor with heart; Bob Grunwell, known as the Ice Man when he was chief sub-editor, a most professional journalist; his side-kick Tom Sheridan, later chief sub-editor, with his ukelele when the occasion was right; Matt Winchester, the dignified production editor who was a fount of local knowledge.

And there was Harry Farrow on the advertising side, who seemed to know everyone in Teesside — at least everyone worth knowing; or his larger-than-life boss, display advertising manager Ken Storry,

agreeable company at any time; John Madden, circulation manager supreme with Joe Livesey his right hand and Joe's son Lol, now transport manager; the talented long-serving artist Ken Coan; Roy Say on the production desk; and Aberdonian George Dunn, a gusting Highland blast when solving newspaper problems, followed by fellow-Aberdonian Bill Yule, a caricature of the canny Scot, whose vast production experience was gained from the shop floor the hard way.

In fact, for a time in the 1970s the *Gazette* had something of a Scottish take-over. The managing director, editor, deputy editor, assistant managing director, production manager and tele-communications manager all hailed from north of the Border. But as a director of Middlesbrough Football Club pointed out, when you look at how many Scots have played for the Boro over the years, the *Gazette* is nothing different. And anyway, the paper was started by a Scot.

The 1970s were not without their difficulties. The *Gazette's* success continued, reflecting the growth of Teesside at the time, but the disaffection and flexing strength of the trade union movement across the country was also felt in Middlesbrough and

The Town Hall and Victoria Square, Middlesbrough, in the 1920s . . . and trams, barrows, bikes and charabancs were the mode of transport of the day. It was through these scenes that Harry Lonsdale eased "Old Faithful", the Gazette's first Model "T" Ford. His son Norman later drove editorial's splendid Morris Cowley.

Now a well-know business guru and TV personality, but in 1970 John Harvey-Jones was chairman of ICI HOC division. Here he shows Frank Sugden, public health inspector, Alderman J. A. Brown, chairman of the health committee, Dr. K. W. Gee, deputy chairman of HOC Division, and M.P. Jim Tinn around the Wilton site.

Before the days of open plan . . . the Gazette newsroom in 1969, with Malcolm Race seated in the centre of the picture pounding out a council report. Tom Sheridan, then deputy Chief Sub-editor, is a visitor from subs and chats to the late Reg Brown. Cathy Mason is the reporter facing the camera. Computer screens were entirely unknown.

Lord Thomson dies

From the *Evening Gazette,* August 4, 1976.

Sadly, the Evening Gazette recorded the death of Lord Thomson of Fleet, chairman of the Thomson Organisation, in a London Hospital in August, 1976. He was 82.

Many leading figures around the world immediately paid tribute:

Sir David Steel, for the Liberal Party, said: "Roy Thomson made a remarkable contribution to the British Press . . . he was an enlightened Press Baron who believed in total editorial freedom".

Lord Goodman, on behalf of the Newspaper Publishers' Association, spoke of Lord Thomson as "this most remarkable man. He exemplified in many ways the best qualities of newspaper proprietorship: a concern for quality, the willingness to leave total freedom to his editors and a business genius that gave employment to many thousands of people".

Lord Thomson of Fleet

After acquiring the Evening Gazette, Lord Thomson took great interest in Teesside. The picture on the left shows Mr Roy Thomson, as he was in 1963, opening a "Focus on Tees-side" exhibition at Thomson House in London.

The Gazette's last old giant ... the Hoe and Crabtree press had stood the paper in good stead for many years. The picture, taken in 1969, shows papers coming off the machines at the rate of 36,000 copies an hour. A quick check and they were carried off to the packers and waiting vans.

both *Gazette* journalists and production staffs were involved in disputes that sometimes led to sanctions and strike action.

The pace of executive change hardly lessened. After six years in the chair, editor Ian Nimmo returned to Edinburgh in 1976 to edit the *Evening News*, the Scottish capital's own newspaper. He was succeeded by Shetlander William "Bill" Sinclair, with a distinguished newspaper pedigree behind him, including the *Daily Telegraph* in London, *The Scotsman*, the old Edinburgh *Evening Dispatch* and the *Evening News*. It

Mr Ian Nimmo, Editor 1970 – 1976

Mr William Sinclair. Editor 1976 – 1982.

Mr David James, Editor 1982 – 1988.

was during Bill Sinclair's editorship that the *Gazette* launched the largest fund-raising project in the paper's history for the life-saving scanner at the new South Cleveland Hospital. Mr John Long, who had been managing the group's Chester centre took over as managing director from Mr Bill Heeps in 1976. It was Mr Long's second career, for he had joined the merchant navy as a young man, and even took his master's certificate, before entering the newspaper world. But a year later he, too, was heading northwards for Edinburgh and Mr T.R.C. Willis, with a management background on the *Economist*, Hong Kong's *South China Morning Post*, the *Belfast Telegraph*, and a former Royal Artillery officer took charge in his place.

By 1982 it was the editor's turn again and Bill Sinclair left on a special group project to be replaced by Mr David James, the deputy editor of the *Evening Post* in Reading. Mr Peter Darling, who had been editor for three years of the *Morning Post* in Sheffield until its closure, then deputy editor of its sister paper, *The Star*, succeeded David James in 1988.

On the management front Mr Tim Willis's 10-year-reign at the *Gazette's* helm ended in 1987 with the appointment of Yorkshireman Mr Tony Hill.

The promise of boom all the way for Teesside, anticipated at its birth in 1966 and throughout the early 70s, had not been maintained. Recession, rising unemployment, deflated industry, boundary changes and general uncertainty took the thrust out of the area. When Teesside booms, the *Gazette,* as we have seen, is alongside with it, when the area flags the *Gazette's* fortunes also shade. During recession, when the market place is weak, it is a time for consolidation, working even harder, sometimes to make little progress, and both Teesside and the *Gazette* for a time found themselves in this situation.

For the paper it was also the start of an on-going period when staff numbers were reduced in all departments due to the recession or the introduction of new working methods.

But reporting the affairs of the area for a century and more also gave the *Gazette* an important sense of perspective. Even when recession hit hardest and the dole queues reached alarming proportions, the *Gazette* knew Teesside would thrive again. There was so much energy, so many skills, so much to offer and such a will to succeed, that the long-term future must be assured — and the *Gazette* began to plan towards that day.

It was managing director Tony Hill, in September, 1988, who buried the time capsule in the enormous hole being dug at the back of Borough Road. The excavations marked the foundations of the hall that would house the *Gazette's* colour press.

It was the biggest and most expensive development in the paper's history, the *Gazette's* stake in the future and the paper's confident commitment and act of faith in the future of Teesside.

Mr Peter Darling, Editor 1988 – 1991.

Mr John Long, Managing Director 1976 – 1977.

Mr Tim Willis, Managing Director 1977 – 1987.

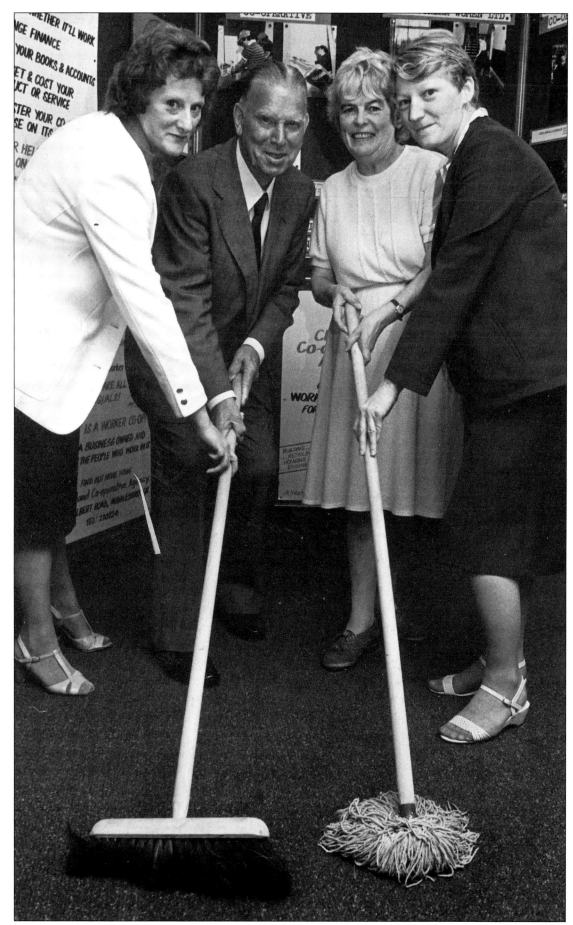

Boro Wonderwomen . . . that's what a group of Mrs Mopps called themselves in 1982 in an effort to land more work. They attended the official opening of Cleveland Co-operative Agency after sweeping and dusting the premises. They are being helped by Middlesbrough's long-serving Labour M.P. at the time, Arthur Bottomley, and Councillor Maureen Taylor. Arthur Bottomley was a good friend of the Evening Gazette and did much to restore trust between his party and the paper after the Kemsley era.

The Campaigner

SOME newspapers are content to publish the news, the advertisements, the important public notices but remain in the main uninvolved in their communities and at a safe distance from their readers. Others create a furore for a short period on a local issue then move on quickly before there is an outcome or retribution.

From the beginning that has never been the way of the *Evening Gazette*. Since its precarious early days, editor by editor for 125 years, the *Gazette* has been a confirmed campaigner on the community's behalf, involved up to the neck with its readers and the problems and aspirations of the area.

The *Gazette* was launched as a campaigning Liberal newspaper with a deep-rooted public conscience because the proprietor felt it was needed at a time of enormous social injustice and deplorable living conditions for the vast majority in the area. He felt that the *Gazette* through its columns could improve the quality of life of the citizens within it.

One of its first campaigns was for a bridge across the Tees at Stockton to improve communications. It never let councils off the rack of investigation by keeping a close watch on how ratepayers' money was spent. It blasted them at the height of the smallpox epidemic of 1870 for the state of sewage facilities in Middlesbrough.

As part of its campaign to improve sanitary conditions of the miners and their families in South Durham, the *Gazette* appointed its own commissioner in 1892 to visit and investigate the situation in the villages. They published more than 30 articles on the subject, but litigation followed an expose in South Hatton and the *Gazette* was brought before Lord Coleridge at Newcastle Assizes and fined £25.

But the *Gazette* had really won the day because it was estimated £250,000 was spent on improving the homes as a result of the paper's campaign. Of course, it helped to establish the *Gazette* as Aukland's "own newspaper" and even during World War 1 it still "covered the area like the evening dew" and battled on behalf of its readers.

In 1905 it was able to tell Teesside that the "Wake Up England" campaign received most attention at the headquarters of England's iron trade and that the evidences of the industrial awakening of Middlesbrough were to be seen on every hand.

Local disasters — down pits, at sea, sometimes national disasters, wherever they struck — for years had seen the *Gazette* trying to rally round and raise funds. Even small campaigns like the paper's Coronation TV Shilling Fund launched in 1953 to provide television sets for children in hospital was a huge success that sent "a glow of pleasure through the heart of every reader". The "Give a Little" campaigns at Christmas to bring cheer to the elderly and needy on Teesside always brought heart-warming responses.

Editor Leslie James led one of the first campaigns to raise funds for hospital equipment and the *Gazette's* "cobalt bomb" cancer treatment machine for North Ormesby Hospital had the area united behind it.

The Teesside artificial kidney unit at North Ormesby, opened in 1969 by Lord Thomson of Fleet, was thanks to the *Evening Gazette* under editor Bill Heeps. He wanted to raise £25,000, but by the generosity of the readers, it finished at nearer £70,000 and one of its features was the steady stream of children to the *Gazette's* office on Saturday mornings, sticky pennies clutched in hands or jam jars clinking with threepenny-bits.

When the horrific Lealholm bus tragedy occurred it was to *Gazette* editor Ian Ninmo that the community turned to be chairman of the Appeal Trust. When editor Bill Sinclair put the *Gazette* behind the Cleveland Scanner Campaign in 1976 to

The original cottage hospital in Middlesbrough was in Dundas Mews and this was the operating theatre complete with fireplace. There are flowers on the table and mantlepiece and the nurse holds a bowl and towel ready for action.

Not a welcoming sight, but the cottage hospital behind the bleak exterior served its purposes well. The Dundas Mews building is now demolished.

A man of standing . . .Dr John Richardson is recorded as the first surgeon of North Ormesby Hospital at the turn of the century.

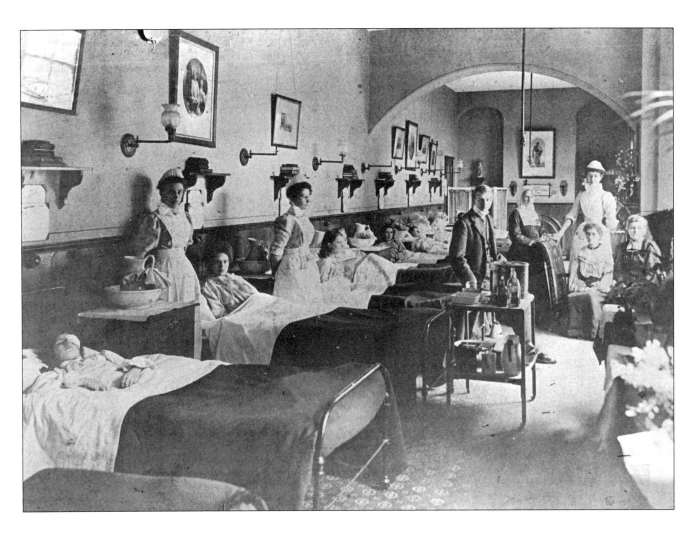

1967: THE STORY THE READERS WROTE TO RAISE £66,669

The year is 1905 and it is the woman's ward in the old North Ormesby Hospital. All the beds are full, the atmosphere is one of starch, not a smile is to be seen, even from the pictures on the walls.

Wanted: £25,000 to save lives

Teesside's artificial kidney unit gets go-ahead: Now it's up to you

IT ALL began on Thursday April 27, 1967, when a first class news story dropped into our laps, writes Terry Donovan.

A woman came to the Evening Gazette's Middlesbrough office to give us a story which was to arouse an astonishing amount of emotion among our readers.

It resulted in an appeal which raised an incredible £66,669 and from now onwards will help to save lives and relieve suffering through Teesside's new Kidney Unit at North Ormesby Hospital.

Readers and paper together . . .the unit was opened by Lord Thomson of Fleet on November 8, 1969.

£50,000 success

And the Kidney Fund strides on

TEESSIDE should have its own ten-bed artificial kidney centre within 18 months.

Eighteen weeks after being launched with a £25,000 target the Evening Gazette's kidney machine fund this weekend passed the £50,000 mark.

Commenting today on the achievement, Ald. J. T. Fletcher, chairman of South Teesside Hospital Management Committee, said: " My first reaction is to congratulate the people of the area in responding to the fund in such a wonderful manner. I should like to thank the Evening Gazette for sponsoring the scheme, and reading so specifically what apparently has been in the minds of Teesside people for some time".

Taking the lead

bring a life-saving whole body scanner to the area many said the £345,000 cost, in spite of a £30,000 donation by ICI, would never be reached.

After five years of fund-raising and hard work more than £700,000 was found and the eight tons of equipment went into immediate use in the battle against cancer in the area.

"Speed the A19!" was the *Gazette's* response to the slow lane attitude of bureaucracy in the late 1960s to a killer road and to improve Teesside's road communications — and things began to happen.

The paper saved the Esk Valley railway line from closure back in the 1970s and commenced a classroom report direct from the children themselves to find out what was happening in Cleveland schools.

It has been on the trail of vandals and drug peddlers, exposed ill treatment to horses exported to the Continent, it has campaigned to tidy up Middlesbrough, improve the environment with Teeswatch and even introduced a touring noise clinic so readers could bring examples of noise pollution to the attention of the authorities.

The *Gazette* has always had a proud record of raising funds and in 1982 a further £40,000 went to Middlesbrough's North Riding Infirmary for a scanner. Two years later £50,000 was being sent to the NSPCC's centenary appeal with the compliments of Teesside. No sooner is a target set, it seems, than it is broken.

More recently, it has campaigned against the takeover of ICI by the Hanson Trust; helped to save that symbol of Teesside, the Transporter Bridge, a famous landmark and important piece of industrial heritage; successfully fought to save the Cleveland Spastic Centre; put smoke alarms in homes; realised the dream of the North Tees Hospital's £600,000 scanner and, as the *Gazette* reaches its 125th year, it is campaigning for funds to build a new children's wing for Butterwick Hospice.

Whether it is in support of the little man against bureaucracy, the weak against the powerful, for the development of Teesside or to safeguard its interests, the *Evening Gazette* has always demonstrated a proud and positive campaigning record from the very beginning.

And the campaign goes on . . .

CLEVELAND SCANNER CAMPAIGN

Docker Jim Dent holds aloft another £2,000 cheque from Middlesbrough Dock Branch of the Transport and General Workers' Union in 1977, one of many contributions for the Gazette-sponsored scanner appeal that raised more than £700,000.

Dream turns to reality for Rita

Cleveland's dream of a residential centre for sufferers of Alzheimer's disease was inspired by one woman who made it her personal mission. The appeal has now raised almost £1 million.

The successful appeal launched in 1991.

o pull together in the best of causes

Surrounded by ducks — army cadets help to sort out the 3,000 "ducks" at the start of a race to raise £750,000 for the 1992 Teesside Hospice Care Foundation Appeal. The target is a 16-bed centre for Teesside. It was the start of many such fund events. funds.

Up to target a year early

WE'VE DONE IT! North Tees health chiefs gave a resounding hoot of success today to celebrate reaching the scanner appeal target — a full year ahead of schedule.

Appeal president, Dr Peter Gill said reaching the £603,000 total was the best Christmas present he and Teesside could have.

● Joy: Celebrating at North Tees Hospital reaching the scanner appeal target are (from left) David Houghton-Roe, Peepa the mascot, appeal chairman Leslie Gilliland, and appeal president Dr Peter Gill.

Another successful scanner appeal completed in 1993

A royal visitor for Leigh Ann ... Sarah Ferguson visits the little girl who lost both legs in a South Bank Road accident, which also killed two other children. The Gazette strongly supported the appeal to provide her with a new life and Teesside was rewarded by its fund-raising efforts when Leech Homes handed over a new home to Leigh Ann and her family.

A good read — even from the top of the new Goss Metroliner colour press in Borough Road. Now the Gazette and its sister papers, like the Herald and Post and South Durham and Teesside Times, are able to print around 5.2 million copies a month and there are around 12 million inserts a year. The front-end technology is almost 100 per cent electronic with state of the art colour scanners in the process department. This is now the Evening Gazette's exciting and very colourful world at the rate of 55,000 copies an hour.

Colourful World

LET THE presses roll!, shouted the editor in the best old Hollywood tradition, especially when his paper had the name of the "real" murderer exclusively blazoned on the front page. The giant presses, roaring out thousands of copies an hour with the latest headlines, have always been symbolic of the power of the Press, a fascination to readers and a thrill even to the journalists.

The *Evening Gazette* is no exception and it has been one of the newspaper's boasts from the outset that it has always had the latest and the best. Without the presses and their skilled crews the newspaper is nothing.

The modern newspaper press is a high-technology engineering wonder to be treated with tender care. It is press problems that cause newspaper disasters and if it is not handled with respect and attention it can react. Some crews believe their presses have personality.

"Crew" is precisely the correct word to describe those who look after its interests. In many ways they are like a ship's company. Preparing the press for another edition is like a new voyage. Ordering a new press is like placing an order for a ship — for it is laid down and built to precise specifications in the best shipbuilding tradition.

The dovetailing production processes in a newspaper have always been complex and, because of the time constraints, often fraught. In the very old days every letter was set by hand from its type case, then painstakingly returned to be ready for the next edition. But then came the revolution of the linotype machine, a steady line of metal "slugs" miraculously spaced, fast and relatively trouble free and the newspaper industry was revolutionised. As soon as they were on the market the *Gazette* bought seven.

Old faithful linotype kept the newspaper in efficient good health for many years, but new computer-controlled technology was progressing around the world, and the days of "hot metal", with its heavy, cumbersome half-drum plates to be man-handled on to the presses, and the pages of lead type made up like giant jigsaws, were well over.

They had served their purpose with distinction, but theirs was a past era and the first of the new wave of computer-based production processes that were to change the entire face and character of the newspaper business was overdue.

Photo-composition was the natural step for the *Evening Gazette* in 1978. In this process hot metal was abandoned, stories and advertisements were set by computer, then output as high-quality images on paper, composed on a paper page, photographed, transferred to a light-sensitive aluminium sheet and was fitted to the press as a flexible, easily-handled plate.

Of course, it was a major milestone in newspaper production and a sensitive time as staffs came to terms with the new process and its impact, yet readers hardly noticed the difference. All the drama of introducing it smoothly was inside the office, with all sides trying to ease the path without disruption in what was one of the biggest newspaper innovations of the century.

But it was only the beginning. The computer age was influencing newspapers just as it was touching businesses and lives in every-day matters around the world. The revolution could not be ignored.

The cautious old production craft unions, which wielded enormous power, sensing that jobs were at stake, had held up the introduction in this country for years. In essence, after journalists had typed their stories and the headlines had been written

The production of a newspaper at the best of times is fraught and complex, but when it is a fast-moving, multi-edition evening paper with a reputation for accuracy and immediacy, then it can be volatile. This is how the Evening Gazette stepped from the past to embrace the computerised present, rediscovered itself in the process and with its new giant colour press and high tec, front-end electronics, it has once more established itself in the forefront of modern newspaper technology.

'The old days and methods were over, the computer revolution could not be ignored'

Roar of the press — the old Hoe and Crabree rotary at full blast. Even in the 1960s, four cylinders were capable of producing 60,000 copies an hour of 32-page papers, using five tons of paper in an hour.

The reel stand on the old rotary press — each reel weighed three-quarters of a ton and contained five miles of paper. Changing a reel on the run or when the paper snapped was a race against time.

and the copy prepared by the sub-editors, it all had to be re-keyed for a second time into the production system by the production staff. Yet the direct-input computerised technology to allow the journalists to send their material directly into the computer system had been in daily use in other countries for years.

The battles between Mr Eddie Shah's newspapers and Mr Rupert Murdoch's *Times, Sunday Times* and *The Sun* at Wapping, which made national headlines, is well enough known, but they had a direct bearing on every newspaper house in Britain. The cost-effectiveness and efficiency of direct input technology, as it was known, immediately put other newspapers at a frightening commercial disadvantage and sad that it was to see so many skilled production workers leave the industry, the inevitability had been understood for a very long time.

Direct input in the shape of PCS screens landed on the desks of the *Evening Gazette* editorial department in 1985. Trepidation reigned, but sound training and the will to make it all happen soon had the journalists well in control of their new-age newspaper system and the challenge was overcome with the minimum of difficulty.

In perspective, the *Gazette* had crashed through a time barrier and found itself in a sophisticated, bright new world of computer technology, full of exciting challenges and possibilities, new fields of potential to be discovered — and for a 116-year-old, a zestful fresh new impetus.

Further major change was not long in arriving. Quietly, hesitatingly, there was talk of the Big One. Wistfully at first, because it did not really seem possible. It was something indefinite, perhaps for the far future. Maybe, sometime, most likely never, some felt. But it was happening elsewhere. There was concern that the *Gazette* could be disadvantaged by competitors. At last it was being talked about openly, seriously, then insistently. We must have full colour.

But Thomson Regional Newspapers Board had already been considering it for their newspapers. In the wake of the computer revolution, the collapse of the trade unions' sway, but in the middle of a world-wide economic recession, when the whole British newspaper industry had never been more volatile, they knew there was a time-frame for action. It was an immense decision.

They knew also the newspapers that would thrive in the future had to be tailored precisely to the needs and demands of readers and advertisers and that the service must be of the highest quality. But did that mean colour? The costs were horrendous. For the group they were frightening. At least £85 million. Could it be afforded? Could it be justified? Could colour be made to work for its money? Was it really necessary? Were there other ways to develop? To their undying credit the Thomson Corporation made their decision with conviction: "Let's go for it", they said.

The *Gazette* might have considered itself down the queue. But they, too, wasted no time. They outlined a case so strong and justified on every front that it was beyond denial. Suddenly the old Crabtree Vickers press, which had given the *Gazette* loyal service, but now with severe limitations for the demands to come, looked jaded and ready for superannuation.

The story of newspapers is full of tales of the improbable that came about or the impossible that happened. There came a whisper that a six-unit, double width full process colour Goss Metroliner press had become available — in South Africa. As colour presses go it had a very colourful background. It had been manufactured in Chicago and shipped to the Argentine just before the Falklands War. The Argentinians took umbridge that the United States was assisting Britain with spy planes. The outcome was that they told the Americans they could stick their press. The deal was off. It was then bought by a Johannesburg company and transported to South Africa, but after installation the company went quickly into liquidation.

A Thomson executive heard the story and flew to Johannesburg, liked what he saw and bought it. And word came winging to Middlesbrough — " It's yours!"

The *Gazette* had pushed ahead by building a new press hall to house their dream machine behind the office in Borough Road. They had to dig deep, 14 metres down to secure the base for the 400-tonne monster. It lay in Southampton docks for nine months before being transported to a warehouse in Billingham for a complete overhaul, where it was found leaked salt

'Quietly, hesitantly, wistfully at first, there was talk of the Big One. Then openly, insistently. . .'

Old days' technology — casting the heavy metal plates to be fitted on to the rotary press. These were the news and advertising pages and it was heavy work. Now the plates are thin, flexible and light.

The Muirhead receiver in the old wire room accepted wired pictures from the main news agencies. Nowadays even the wire room has gone and picture selection is by computer on the editorial floor.

At first it looked like Roman remains behind the Gazette office, but the big dig was to secure the foundations of the new 400-tonne colour press and make it secure.

Start drilling! Once before when a new press was installed vibration ruined the beer in the next-door-hotel. This time no chances were taken and the base went down 14 metres.

water on its voyage from South America had damaged cylinders and other working parts.

The *Evening Gazette's* colour press was commissioned on July 6, 1989, and Mr Michael Brown, president of the Thomson Corporation, flew over from New York for the honour of pressing the starter button. It was historic. The *Evening Gazette* once more was in the forefront of newspaper technology, a first in Thomson's in mainland Britain and once more breaking new ground in the regional newspaper field with full colours flying.

The new press was given a name, "The President", to mark the Thomson president's visit. Mr Brown told captains of Teesside industry that the *Gazette* was now a born-again newspaper for a born-again area.

"The people of Teesside have shown how they can pick themselves up and this is the place to be", he said. "This is a great newspaper, serving a great area and both are heading for the good times. Our prosperity depends on the prosperity of the area we serve. We know that this area and the *Gazette* are winners".

They were words which echoed yet again from the old days, the fortunes of the *Gazette* and its Teesside community inextricably linked.

Managing director Neil Burnett and editor Peter Darling could hardly believe their good fortune to have been in office and have the paper in their safekeeping at such an historic moment. Now it was time to roll up sleeves and make it work.

Yet still dramatic development continued. The paper plunged into all the new technologies in every direction, the editorial department, in particular, embracing the latest in editing and design and transmission systems. And it was also decided to add facilities the following year to enable the new colour press to run in excess of 400,000 inserts a week, from A4 to tabloid size, to give the *Gazette* yet another first in its field.

And so the colourful wonder came about and the newspaper is at the forefront of computer technology in this country and confronts the future with optimism and from strength. Sir Hugh Gilzean Reid would have been astounded — and proud. After all, out front is where he always wanted his paper to be.

Modern Times

THE anticipation of colour printing was matched only by the reality. The *Gazette* had stepped into a new world. Hugh Gilzean Reid's words at the launch of the paper in 1889 about embarking upon his bold adventure had come full cycle. Now it was a new, bold and colourful adventure.

It was not the fact of colour alone and the extra dimension it created that was the only importance — it was also the opportunity made available to undertake the kind of developments that had once been only dreams. From 1989 onwards the *Gazette* was in a position to go hunting for opportunity.

Like every adventure the successful conclusion has to be worked for. Teesside was still gripped by recession, the dole queue was 38,000 workers long, the economy pancake-flat, the traditional big industrial employers were rocked to their foundations, shipbuilding had gone and the fiercest kind of competition was rampant within the media. But from its beginning days the *Gazette* knew how to rough-and-tumble for survival.

In fact, battle had already been engaged and the *Gazette* was in the ascendancy. In the previous two years of preparation for the new press, the company had been making substantial progress in several directions. It had even re-introduced the *Sports Gazette*, after its closure in 1983, and launched the *Darlington Evening Gazette* in the wake of the demise of the old Darlington *Evening Dispatch* and because predatory incursions had been attempted into the *Gazette's* patch. The paper had also invested heavily in the sponsorship of such local institutions as Middlesbrough Football Club, the Little Theatre, the Forum, Middlesbrough Festival and Cleveland Arts.

Now it threw itself into making its colour press work for its living. But the modern colour press, as we have seen, is a complex state of the art technology giant which meant production staff had to reach even higher standards of technical expertise. It also meant addressing the design and look of the paper. Editorial and advertising staff were therefore immediately involved in learning new skills and approaches, not least becoming aware of the new opportunities — and something that had never happened before, contract printing services were offered to outsiders.

The learning curve for all departments was almost vertical. Thinking colour was a

Mr Tony Hill, Managing Director 1987 - 1989

Mr Neil J.M. Burnett, Managing Director 1989 - 1991

Mr Warwick Brindle, Managing Director 1991 - 1994

new experience. In many respects it called for deserting the old traditional approaches and disciplines. But that old axiom of re-inforcing strength was also understood and resources previously unavailable were suddenly the order of the day. And all the activity was designed to meet one, clear-cut, prime objective — the highest quality service in everything for the customer.

Mr Neil J.M. Burnett, another Aberdonian, who had been the assistant managing director of Thomson Regional Newspaper's Cardiff centre, was given the role to maximise the development.

Of course, the great demand of daily newspapers is that all these tasks have to be undertaken without interruption or any kind of diminution of service or quality. Indeed, readers expect and deserve only the best. And, therefore, while taking aboard all the training and new thinking in almost everything, the *Gazette* simultaneously still had to thunder out, edition by edition, the latest with the best, as its founder had decreed. Perhaps it was not unexpected — because the trick of good journalism is to have your ear to the ground and be at the right place at the right time — but the world exclusive scoop of the "Iraqi Supergun" story at Teesport by reporter Ron Livingston, which reverberated throughout the corridors of Westminster power, was still a major fillip for the paper and its staff along with a clutch of other editorial and advertising awards, including the Samuel Storey Editorial Award to editor Peter Darling.

Mr Warwick Brindle took over as managing director of the paper in August 1991, when Neil Burnett moved on to the Reading centre, and in his first year Mr Brindle was able to report dramatic changes in the company's fortunes.

With a circulation and marketing background in Burnley and Blackburn and at Thomson Regional Newspapers' headquarters, and a former assistant managing director in Newcastle and managing director in Chester, Warwick Brindle was well qualified and experienced to take on the task of developing the business and breaking new ground for the paper.

In perspective, 1991 was a year of enormous significance for the *Gazette*. The appointment of Mr Ranald Allan as editor in July 1991 added further impetus. Yet another Aberdonian Scot, he began his career on the *Evening Express* in his native city, transferred to its sister paper, the *Press & Journal*, Britain's oldest daily newspaper, as assistant to the editor, before being appointed senior assistant editor of *The Scotsman* in Edinburgh. For a time he was seconded as executive editor of the new *Scotland on Sunday*, before being appointed editor of the Evening Post in Reading. He arrived on Teesside with a reputation of professionalism, getting things done and increasing circulation.

It was the year in which the newspaper, securing its own base and future prosperity, took over its arch rival, the Reeds Times Group. It may have come as a shock, but it declared loud and clear that the *Gazette* meant business. And to add delight to the paper's new optimism in 1991 the drift in circulation, which had continued for years, was arrested.

Reeds, in the shape of the *Teesside Times*,

Mr Ranald Allan, appointed Editor in 1991

Customs swoop on Tees

GUN RUN TO IRAQ IS FOILED

How the Gazette exclusively brought the news to the world.

She came, she saw . . . and walked in the wilderness, complete with handbag. But as Lady Thatcher strolled over the old Head Wrightson works she could also envisage it as a major development site for the future to set the tone for the re-vitalisation of Teesside. And as she predicted, in her footsteps the new industries arise.

The Gazette management team as the paper reaches its 125th year, with Lord Thomson, chairman of International Thomson, at its head, during a visit to Teesside. From left to right: editor Ranald Allan, managing director Warwick Brindle, financial controller David Howarth, Lord Thomson, newspaper sales and promotions manager Steve Walker, telephone sales manager Karen Owens, production director Bob Ramage and marketing manager Jane Nugent.

launched at the begining of the prosperous 70s, had been a thorn in the *Gazette's* side, competing commercially for every centimetre of advertising space. But when the acquisition became possible to the satisfaction of both companies, the *Gazette's* position was further strengthened and in spite of the impact of such an event, the integration was carried through smoothly and quickly.

The way ahead was becoming clear to everyone. The investment in the colour press, the investment in electronic editing and general computerisation, the investment in people and the manner in which all these new-found resources were utilised was paying dividends. The *Gazette* was re-establishing itself again as the number one regional newspaper on Teesside with increasing influence far beyond its own boundaries.

From its increasing power-base, a further perspective became clear. With such excellent colour facilities and production and editorial flexibility, not enjoyed by many of the *Gazette's* competitors, the ground was now clear to invest in new products. This, too, was clarifying as the shape of things to come.

So as the country continued in recession,

The expanding North Eastern Evening Gazette . . . just some of the titles now being produced from Borough Road.

and while others stood back waiting for more propitious times, the *Gazette's* new leaders took the bold decision to invest and expand into new markets. With such a major decision made, there was only one approach — accelerate into it in top gear with enthusiasm and energy. Perhaps there has never been a period of such pel-mel, helter-skelter, headlong, dynamic development since the paper was founded. It was demanding, it was exciting, it was invigorating, it was breath-taking. New editions, late

Telling the world . . . Teesside 2000 is a Gazette initiative and business up-date that presents an accurate and positive image of the area, designed to win investment. It is sent quarterly to key decision-makers throughout the world.

and early, the launch of *Gazette Local,* weekly community news inserts, *Saturday Sports Preview,* the *Holiday Directory*, visitors' guides, *Cars Quarterly,* home and wedding specials, new looks at design, then re-design again to keep it fresh, the introduction of big, eye-catching graphics, sections aimed carefully at specific areas of the market then tailored and fine-tuned to further meet their needs, ideas sparking and, at the same time, major refurbishments and new layouts throughout the building to free staff to do their jobs in the best circumstances and to take heed of the massive investment in computer technology.

Among those new launches was also the prestigious *Teesside 2000*, a major quality publication aimed at presenting Teesside to the world as a further promotional aid to investment in the area. In fact, *Teesside 2000* circulates the world to reach the business leaders who matter and the decision-makers who might be tempted to try Teesside. It is a first class demonstration of the kind of initiative that built the area in the first place, self-help of the highest order, once more newspaper and community working in tandem, and the *Gazette* received justified praise from the business community, local MPs — and even a laudatory House of Commons motion for its effort.

By the end of 1992, the *Gazette* was walking on air with the best general performance in the history of the paper. It started the year with seven branded products and finished with seventeen. And the development continues.

Teesside is also once more on the move. Now with a university, the consolidated steel-producing centre of Britain, the most modern in Europe, the energy power base of the UK, including a gas plant, new modern industries developing out of the old, tourism a potential new major industry, supported by new marinas, the Maritime Museum, heritage centres, the huge investment along the Tees up to Yarm, which will transform the riverside into a Thames-like visitors' delight of leisure pursuits and the many other developments that are changing the face of the area. Once again there is excitement as ways are examined to realise its vast potential as Teesside looks to the future.

There is excitement too at the *Gazette* where, days before this book's deadline, it was announced that managing director Warwick Brindle was moving to Edinburgh to become managing director of the Thomson Regional Newspaper flagship company, The Scotsman Publications Limited.

As the *Evening Gazette* celebrates its 125th birthday and welcomes a new managing director, the words spoken at the inauguration of the paper's colour press have never been so apt — "a born again newspaper in a born again area".

INVESTORS IN PEOPLE

The Evening Gazette not only makes an investment in the community, but also in its employees. It has prestigiously been judged by the Teesside Economic Council as an "Investor in People", recognising the valuable contribution our employees make towards our business. The Gazette is also committed to upholding the exacting standards and principles of "Investors in People".

Evening Gazette

A newspaper rooted in its community for 125 years and beyond

Into the future . . . Teesside's young faces of tomorrow are already familiar with their Evening Gazette. This is the next generation of Teessider who will take the newspaper and the area into the 21st century and beyond.

The picture was taken at the launch of a newspaper in education scheme, based on the Evening Gazette, at Brambles Farm Primary School. It is aimed to help children of all abilities as well as ethnic groups. In the background is the teacher co-ordinating the project, Satti Collins, the editor, and student teacher Hazel Boocock.

A face of the Gazette that readers do not always see. . . editor Ranald Allan makes a special call to see Leigh-Ann Johns, the little girl who lost both legs in a tragic road accident, to present her with a framed Gazette photograph of the day the Duchess of York came to visit her in hospital.

Into the 21st century

AS THE *Evening Gazette* reaches its century-and-a-quarter and now looks forward to entering the second millennium it is a time to take stock. For longer than anyone can remember, before the dawn of the 20th century or aeroplanes flew or the Boro first kicked a ball, the *Gazette* has been the voice of Teesside.

It has been an organ of record, faithfully chronicling events, pointing the way of change yet simultaneously often its instrument at a time of volatile and unprecedented change.

When Hugh Gilzean Reid launched his hopeful little newspaper with the high ideals in 1869, how in his time warp could he have envisaged flights to London in less than an hour, that man was destined to walk on the moon or that a box in the corner would present moving pictures in colour as they happen?

Even to suggest such ravings would have produced calls for a straightjacket or fingers tapping heads.

So who can anticipate what changes will stem from this age of science and computers in the new bold adventures ahead? The innovations and great deeds of the *Gazette's* past were accomplished by the leaders and staffs of the past and the *Gazette* has always been fortunate in the calibre of those who worked on it.

They have set a great newspaper tradition of professionalism, dedication and innovation with a scintillating list of firsts in its field — the first halfpenny evening newspaper in Britain; the first in the North-east to use steam presses; a pioneer of sporting journalism; pioneer of the late news "box"; first newspaper to develop a results scoreboard at football matches; a pioneer of colour printing and insert publications.

It is a legacy and heritage that the paper regards with pride and it will be carried forward.

Not only has the *Evening Gazette* survived all those years where many of its competitors failed, but it has also thrived. And that is indeed an achievement.

So today with its space-age technology and big colour press the *Evening Gazette* is placed firmly to look forward to the adventures to come from a position of strength and with anticipation. One thing is certain — it will be leading from the front.

But inextricably it is also linked to the fortunes of Teesside. Over the last 125 years newspaper and community have shared the journey together, the good and the rough, with the same objectives and the same sense of destiny.

Now once more Teesside pushes forward with the old energy and thrust to realise its potential. And that is how both will stride confidently — and still with some bold adventuring — into the 21st century together.

Subscribers

PRESENTATION COPIES

1 Lord Thomson of Fleet • 2 Mayor of Middlesbrough • 3 Mayor of Stockton
4 Mayor of Langbaurgh • 5 Cleveland County Library • 6 Evening Gazette
7 Michael Brown • 8 R C Hall • 9 Gordon Paul • 10 R Kiernan • 11 Stuart Garner
12 Warwick Brindle • 13 Ranald Allan • 14 R A Ramage • 15 David C Howarth
16 Gary Fearon • 17 Steve Walker • 18 Jane Nugent • 19 Christine Pearce
20 Ian Nimmo • 21 Bill Heeps • 22 Bill Sinclair • 23 Michael Morrissey

24	D Granycome	66	F D Stewart Davison	108	M A Ruane
25	P Harris	67	H Stuckert	109	P Wormald
26	J K Heward	68	K Armstrong	110	G Ford
27	M Hill	69	E Condon	111	S A Anderson
28	J Horsley	70	A Ferst	112	A Anderson
29	J Kelly	71	K Newton	113	D Bates
30	I Laing	72	A Sims	114	K A Bell
31	R Livingstone	73	T Argument	115	N J Briston
32	H Logan	74	J A Barnard	116	C Burdon
33	D Lorimer	75	A Coverdale	117	J L Corner
34	K Magee	76	A Gallant	118	P Daniel
35	M McGeary	77	G Poole	119	A K Boughey
36	A McKenzie	78	E A Quinn	120	S Elworthy
37	M Morgan	79	M J Whitwell	121	G Fairbairn
38	N Morrison	80	L Atkinson	122	E Paylor
39	S L Nicholson	81	D Ball	123	M Spence
40	F O'Reardon	82	K Bennett	124	A Vickers
41	M Passant	83	P D Boyle	125	A Wilkinson
42	J Paul	84	K Davies	126	B Thompson
43	M Pickering	85	M P Derengowski	127	P Turner
44	M Potter	86	A Farn	128	J M Ashford
45	G Robertson	87	D Grounds	129	S Elliott
46	D Robson	88	P Karlsson	130	D Jamieson
47	D Spaldin	89	M Karlsson	131	M Jones
48	A Todd	90	G Phillips	132	T M Maddison
49	V Vandenbroecke	91	S Rennie	133	I McIntyre
50	C Fenn	92	P Ryan	134	J D Moody
51	L Romaine	93	D Smart	135	T Reed
52	V J Coulson	94	T Smart	136	C Robertson
53	N Abbott	95	N Smith	137	B Robinson
54	D Bohill	96	D Taylor	138	J Jelly
55	D P Browning	97	P Walker	139	E J Johnson
56	S Calverts	98	S Forbes	140	C McGrother
57	B Edwards	99	R Hill	141	D Whinyates
58	A D Gallon	100	K A Hunter	142	L Brady
59	P Gannon	101	K Sinton	143	V Dickinson
60	P J Gray	102	A Dumphy	144	J Dixon
61	D J Irvin	103	A Johnston	145	P Grainger
62	A Levett	104	P Montellier	146	S J Fisher
63	A Little	105	K Taylor	147	D Homer
64	S Race	106	G Cowton	148	C Hughes
65	M Robson	107	D Hutchinson	149	G Hunter

150 J Jorgensen	207 W Malcolm	264 K Trimble
151 C McCraith	208 L L Morrison	265 J Tweddell
152 E Myers	209 A Sanderson	266 T Verrill
153 E Pickering	210 A Allen	267 Y G White
154 M Roberts	211 P Barr	268 M Whitfield
155 M Storey	212 P Farrow	269 P F Whittle
156 J Wilson	213 P Haley	270 G Cuthbert
157 S Alderson	214 R Hill	271 P McAvoy
158 J D Ball	215 T Marritt	272 E Nelson
159 A T Evans	216 W Rowlands	273 N Owens
160 M Harris	217 K M Ainsworth	274 C Rees
161 A Laird	218 J Devenport	275 S Rees
162 E Marston	219 C Dyball	276 E Surtees
163 T J Shildrick	220 J Gray	277 L Aston
164 N Sioutis	221 C Hurry	278 S L Bowman
165 N Ditchburn	222 R M Owens	279 J Grainger
166 A Smith	223 P D Race	280 B Haswell
167 A Ward	224 P Terry	281 C Hutt
168 G Ashen	225 G Thomas	282 C McDonald
169 C Brain	226 J Walshaw	283 J McGuinness
170 I Clennett	227 A Cook	284 L Overton
171 M Cook	228 G Harwood	285 S Powell
172 M Davies	229 J Batey	286 T Tate
173 F Dobbs	230 S Burns	287 J Thompson
174 L Fraser	231 J A Byrne	288 J E Usher
175 G D Harris	232 N Coulton	289 P Walker
176 N Hill	233 J Dixon	290 S I Allan
177 K Johnston	234 A Dowling	291 E Broatch
178 T McNeill	235 D R Durant	292 A C Cape
179 S Pearson	236 M Freeman	293 L Grandi
180 C Russell	237 D Ghosh	294 S Hanson
181 A Scott	238 E Grainger	295 M Kent
182 A Smith	239 N Green	296 L Liddement
183 T Tyerman	240 J Halliday	297 S A Murray
184 J Coates	241 I Harbron	298 G Ross
185 J Dinsdale	242 C Hesse	299 T Wardley
186 C Ford	243 C Holliday	300 K A Alderson
187 M Gowling	244 J Hunton	301 C Lister
188 M Holt	245 J Hutchinson	302 A Snell
189 J Martin	246 V Jackson	303 S Anderson
190 M McGlynn	247 D Jenkins	304 L Banks
191 V L Millward	248 D Johnson	305 V L James
192 S A Oxley	249 T M Littlefair	306 A Lewis
193 C Riddle	250 P Lundy	307 H Smith
194 L Sparkes	251 J Marsh	308 E J Wilson
195 J Todd	252 M A Medley	309 P Hall
196 L Hannon	253 K Mellor	310 S Kirby
197 A Livingston	254 P S Midgley	311 M McClure
198 S R MacCallum	255 Y N Mitchell	312 V Bentley
199 M C McClachlan	256 J Moore	313 S Brown
200 H E Rylatt	257 J Munkley	314 S Catterall
201 L Wilgaus	258 J Myers	315 J A Knox
202 E Flett	259 K Owens	316 B Lambert
203 P Ford	260 L Pearson	317 M Leonard
204 B Goddard	261 J Penman	318 H D Small
205 J Harris	262 K Pennock	319 D C Stapleton
206 A Lambert	263 M Smith	320 A Everton

321 C Havelock	378 G McCamphill	435 M T Kelly
322 C Holloway	379 K Padgett	436 T Lillystone
323 P Lipthorpe	380 R Shields	437 M Newton
324 M Oliver	381 P L Billau	438 L Patton
325 K Ruddick	382 P Davies	439 V Pearcy
326 G Shields	383 P Delplanque	440 M Pearson
327 M Silcox	384 P Hart	441 K Saddington
328 M Taylor	385 M Havelock	442 J Scott
329 R Tiffney	386 S James	443 J L Thompson
330 N Williams	387 L Melvin	444 J Ward
331 T Young	388 A Pickin	445 P Watson
332 V L Allen	389 J Sullock	446 J Danks
333 J Alsop	390 J Williams	447 D Routh
334 P Alsop	391 D I Wright	448 B Shirt
335 J P Carter	392 A Birch	449 M Bowen
336 J Cowen	393 P Coulson	450 M T Farrow
337 S Crisp	394 A Cutler	451 L Grylls
338 A Donavan	395 L Jones	452 T Hartley
339 T Donovan	396 P LeFevre	453 A Laing
340 E Hoggarth	397 J Stevens	454 A Nicholson
341 I Leahy	398 T M Kay	455 P A Rak
342 E Lipthorpe	399 J Flynne	456 T Robson
343 J Lipthorpe	400 A Jefferies	457 J A M Simper
344 S A Llewellyn	401 A C Davison	458 J Spink
345 P Ludley	402 K G Gatley	459 I T Thirkeld
346 A Parr	403 J Gilbert	460 J Walker
347 S Pollard	404 C E Glasgow	461 P C Wright
348 N C Prest	405 J Nugent	462 P Alsop
349 L Shields	406 J Smith	463 A Kettlewell
350 E M Taylor	407 M Medley	464 A Thompson
351 B Walker	408 W Brindle	465 D Coombs
352 G Downes	409 E Connor	466 P Crooks
353 L Love	410 R Conyard	467 L Donovan
354 B A Robinson	411 F Coupland	468 K Dryden
355 A Darling	412 K Dale	469 D Heward
356 J Fernie	413 R Gent	470 D Burke
357 D J Glynn	414 S A Groom	471 J Carter
358 A Gray	415 G A Kelley	472 G Hobson
359 S Jackson	416 G Kulscar	473 R Nutsford
360 P J Miller	417 L Livesey	474 K Pugh
361 V Truefitt	418 J May	475 O Poole
362 T M Baggott	419 P Millward	476 J Barron
363 T J Clennett	420 M Prest	477 R Masterson
364 J Cox	421 G Reed	478 R Havelock
365 E Doyle	422 S Rooney	479 J Manning
366 M Merifield	423 J Brown	480 A Brack
367 D Vipond	424 C L Brown	481 G Mount
368 S M Withrington	425 S E Burnett	482 F Boswell
369 E Cassidy	426 J Carberry	483 P Coleman
370 D Creed	427 V Carter	484 J E Hanson
371 G T Lowther	428 M J Dean	485 A Bointon
372 G P Pinkney	429 H Eccles	486 L Johnston
373 D A Ramrekha	430 S Geddes	487 J Putson
374 S Ramshaw	431 C Gill	488 R Holliday
375 P Skipp	432 B Green	489 J Salt
376 S Ford	433 K Hatfield	490 A Whitwell
377 J Kerr	434 J L Johnson	491 M Wilson

492 J T Coburn	549 Joan Hawksby	606 Alan Curry
493 A Connor	550 Mrs Salmon	607 James Shaw
494 S Crown	551 Mr F J Brown	608 Mr R Yale
495 C M A Fenton	552 Doris Gardiner	609 Anthony Miller
496 L Gent	553 Colin Preston	610 Mrs G Trainor
497 M R K Golden	554 Sean Callaghan	611 Emma Thompson
498 M Hood	555 Stephen Horner	612 Kenneth Clewes
499 A Proudman	556 Mrs S Davies	613 Mr Arthur Hodds
500 S E Robinson	557 Maureen Corden	614 John Harrison
501 L Spearen	558 Norman Smart	615 William Westgarth
502 C K Watson	559 Thomas Coulton	616 Mr Leslie Sparrow
503 C R Wearmouth	560 Mrs Whitfield	617 Mr William Salkeld
504 E Wilson	561 Mr Urwin	618 James Everall
505 B Adamson	562 Gerald Dougan	619 James Everall
506 A Tweddle	563 Joseph Howse	620 Mrs C McNamara
507 R Chedzey	564 Eric Hewitson	621 Dr John Forbes
508 K Mylan	565 Eric Hewitson	622 Mr George Reynolds
509 T Young	566 Kenneth Lake	623 Mrs Gladys Whatton
510 S Hawkins	567 Marjorie Tidy	624 Thelma Bean
511 G Nicholson	568 Veronica Plews	625 Norman Yandle
512 A Akbar	569 Mr Leslie Fiddes	626 Ken Bibby
513 A Beg	570 Mr Ronald Frank	627 James Wilson
514 T A Bell	571 Moira Williams	628 Amy Bartram
515 E Brown	572 Moira Williams	629 Maureen Tood
516 J Carroll	573 Brian Cunnington	630 Maureen Tood
517 D Cooper	574 Enid & Goff Wilson	631 Cliff Crosskill
518 A Hallet	575 William Gibson	632 Glenys Levitt
519 C Hudson	576 William Davies	633 William Slingsby
520 S Hudson	577 William Davies	634 Valerie Watkins
521 S J Hunter	578 William Davies	635 Michael Crossen
522 V Kirby	579 Norman Pickthall	636 Harold Thompson
523 S Kirby	580 William Salter	637 Mrs V York
524 J E McCormick	581 Malcolm Westerman	638 Stephen Whitehouse
525 B Newton	582 Gerard Burns	639 Cyril Bailey
526 A Richards	583 Gerard Burns	640 John Yellow
527 C Richardson	584 Gerard Burns	641 Nigel Gibb
528 C Taylor	585 Norman Oxley	642 Mrs Lincoln
529 K Thompson	586 Jim McLaren	643 Mr Charles Donovan
530 A D Tosh	587 Margaret McCormick	644 Mrs Lonsdale
531 J Widdowson	588 Cliff Summers	645 Mr T Nicholls
532 M Appleyard	589 Alan Campion	646 Mrs P Duffy
533 T Barker	590 Ivor Davies	647 Mr B Dixon
534 G M Bell	591 Thomas Wood	648 Mrs D Harris
535 R Brophy	592 Robert Foster	649 Miss E Yeoman
536 Dennis Hooton	593 Joan Southall	650 Mr D Nellist
537 Margaret Manders	594 Margaret Andrew	651 Mr G A McDonnell
538 John Whittingham	595 Margaret Andrew	652 Mr A Watts
539 Margaret Chandler	596 Margaret Andrew	
540 Sophie Eggermont	597 Margaret Andrew	
541 James Hill	598 Margaret Andrew	
542 Leo Banks	599 Margaret Andrew	
543 Howard Fleming	600 Margaret Andrew	
544 Alan Foxton Reeve	601 Margaret Andrew	
545 Janet Smith	602 James Briggs	
546 Janet Smith	603 John Dixon	
547 Norman Moorsom	604 Jack Hornby	
548 Sheila Smith	605 Ronald Hornby	